SIGNALBOXES

for the Modeller

Michael A Vanns

Ian Allan PUBLISHING

First published 2011

ISBN 978 0 7110 3501 0

Published by Ian Allan Publishing

An imprint of Ian Allan Publishing Ltd, Hersham, Surrey, KT12 4RG
Printed in England by Ian Allan Printing Ltd, Hersham, Surrey, KT12 4RG

Code: 1107/x

Distributed in the United States of America and Canada by BookMasters Distribution Services

Visit the Ian Allan Publishing website at *www.ianallanpublishing.com*

ABOVE The Saxby & Farmer signalbox provided for the SER at Wateringbury in 1893. *I. J. Stewart*

TITLE PAGE A 'Cumbrian Mountain Express' headed by SR 4-6-0 No 850 *Lord Nelson* passes the MR signalbox at Wennington Junction during the summer of 1984. *Author*

MIX
Paper from responsible sources
FSC® C014615

CONTENTS

Introduction

After the passing of the Regulation of Railways Act 1889 every line in Great Britain over which passenger trains travelled had to be controlled under Absolute Block regulations. That meant keeping spaces – designated sections of track – clear between trains travelling in the same direction on the same line. To achieve this, trusted staff called signalmen had to regulate the entry and exit of trains through the section of track they controlled by co-operating with their colleagues on either side. They did this by exchanging coded messages tapped out on bells and gongs and by manipulating special electrical equipment, called block instruments, that indicated the state of the line and whether or not trains were travelling in their section. For controlling trains that might run in either direction over single-track lines, special block instruments were devised from which physical reminders of a train's right to occupy a section could be issued and received. These 'tokens' could take the form of short sticks (staffs), disc-shaped tablets or, after 1914, large metal keys. For any other messages that needed to be communicated between signalmen, single-needle electric telegraph instruments were used, supplemented or in some cases superseded at the very end of the 19th century by telephones.

To allow trains in and out of sections, signalmen operated mechanical levers working semaphore signals, and the Regulation of Railways Act 1889 required that these be interlocked with all points/turnouts on the main running lines so that no train could be signalled over a route that was not correctly set for it. The place

ABOVE Petts Wood Box (on the LCDR) seems an appropriate name for a structure resembling an outsize dog kennel. The application of the timber cladding provides a good example of weatherboarding. *D. Cullum*

where all this activity occurred, where all the electrical and mechanical equipment was located, was called a signalbox. Some railway companies used the term 'signal cabin', but for the majority of signalmen – in fact for most railway staff anywhere in the country – the abbreviation 'box' was almost universally understood to be where signalmen spent their days [**1**]. The term could have had its origins with the mechanical telegraphs of the late 18th and early 19th centuries, although 'station' seems to have been a more common suffix for the words 'signal', 'semaphore' and 'telegraph' in connection with these installations. It is still somewhat puzzling as to why 'signal hut' or 'signal house' did not become the preferred terminology for railway usage, as the naming of pre-signalbox signalling installations (i.e. pre-1860) had been descriptive of the structures being referred to, i.e. signalling 'platform', signalling 'stage' and signal 'tower'. For such an important railway control centre for the regulation of train movements, the word 'box' still seems almost derogatory.

No matter what the origins of the nomenclature, if you are modelling passenger trains running in and out of a terminal station or along a stretch of track, either single or with lines dedicated to trains only running in one direction where there are turnouts or sidings, and you have chosen to set the scene sometime between 1889 and about 1960, you will need to provide a signalbox.

If you push the date back to 1870 you will still need a recognisable signalbox if you have a stretch of main line with turnouts, but it could be a smaller structure than that of a decade later. On a secondary branch line, be it single- or double-track, you could get away with a few levers in the open air next to a small wooden or brick-built hut with some form of heating. At a single-line station you would not even need the hut, any communication equipment in the form of electric telegraph instruments (no electric token instruments until after 1874) being in the main station buildings.

Move your date back again to between 1860 and 1870, and although termini and other large stations each had a signalbox (or a number of small 'boxes) the only other location where you would need one for authenticity would be at a junction between passenger lines. Prior to 1860 you are relieved of any obligation, because the structures did not exist. At stations there would be levers only where there were turnouts and perhaps a single-post 'station' semaphore with two arms – one each for signalling trains into and out of the station [**2**]. At junctions there might be some form of raised platform – or stage – with a hut, exposed levers and a couple of posts carrying a pair of semaphores each. But if you are modelling the pre-1860s British railway scene you are truly in a minority and have to be (or probably are) more than an expert in early signalling.

For the majority of modellers, of course, the period chosen will be somewhere between 1923 and 1968. In this timeframe, and no matter what part of the country you model, there will be few excuses for not including at least one signalbox on your layout. From the 1960s, and if you model the diesel and electric era, you can have colour-light signals and avoid having to provide a

ABOVE The GNR's 1880 signalbox at Little Steeping was gently slipping into the Lincolnshire Fens when this photograph was taken in the summer of 1980. Notice how its inclination was adjusted to compensate for the lean when the chimney stack was rebuilt. In model form, a signalbox at this angle would be something special. *Author*

LEFT The signal hut and double-arm station semaphore at the NBR's Belses station, illustrating a signalling arrangement typical in the days before signalboxes were equipped with interlocked lever frames and block instruments. *Author's collection*

Abbreviations

The following recognised abbreviations for Britain's railways (and regions of British Railways) are used in this book:

- **BR** British Railways
- **CR** Caledonian Railway
- **ER** Eastern Region
- **FR** Furness Railway
- **GCR** Great Central Railway
- **GER** Great Eastern Railway
- **GNR** Great Northern Railway
- **GNSR** Great North of Scotland Railway
- **GSWR** Glasgow & South Western Railway
- **GWR** Great Western Railway
- **HBR** Hull & Barnsley Railway
- **HR** Highland Railway
- **LBSCR** London, Brighton & South Coast Railway
- **LCDR** London, Chatham & Dover Railway
- **LMR** London Midland Region
- **LMS** London, Midland & Scottish Railway
- **LNER** London & North Eastern Railway
- **LNWR** London & North Western Railway
- **LSWR** London & South Western Railway
- **LTSR** London, Tilbury & Southend Railway
- **LYR** Lancashire & Yorkshire Railway
- **MGNJR** Midland & Great Northern Joint Railway
- **MR** Midland Railway
- **MSLR** Manchester, Sheffield & Lincolnshire Railway
- **NBR** North British Railway
- **NER** North Eastern Railway or (from 1948) North Eastern Region
- **NSR** North Staffordshire Railway
- **SDJR** Somerset & Dorset Joint Railway
- **SECR** South Eastern & Chatham Railway
- **SER** South Eastern Railway
- **SR** Southern Railway or (from 1948) Southern Region
- **ScR** Scottish Region
- **TVR** Taff Vale Railway
- **WR** Western Region

signalbox by arguing that your terminus or stretch of track is controlled remotely from a signalling centre, miles away in the fiddle yard or on another baseboard.

This is not an instructional book telling you how to scratch-build a model or what materials to use. That aspect is well covered in a number of readily available books or DVDs. Nor does it provide a definitive list of all the currently available ready-made, plastic or card kits. What this work will do is help you determine where a model signalbox should be located on your layout, what it should look like (depending on when you are claiming it was built and by whom and what period you are modelling), what equipment it should contain (if you are prepared to go that far to achieve authenticity) and what there should be immediately surrounding your structure. Hopefully, it will inspire you and draw attention to those characteristics that can make or break the authentic 'look' of your signalbox [**3**].

Bibliography

BOOKS AND MAGAZINES

British Railway Modelling No 1: Lineside Buildings, Paul Bason (Warners Group Publications, 2007)

British Railway Modelling No 4: Scratch-Built Buildings, Paul Bason, (Warners Group Publications, 2008)

Modelling Buildings: Methods and Materials, Malcolm J. Smith (Pendon Museum Trust Ltd, 2003)

Signal Boxes of the London & South Western Railway, G. A. Pryer (Oakwood Press, 2000)

The Signal Box, Signalling Study Group (OPC, 1986)

The Silver Link Library of Railway Modelling: Creating the Scenic Landscape, Trevor Booth (Silver Link, 1994)

Model Railway Constructor No 4: Buildings, Chris Leigh (Ian Allan, 1982)

DVDs

British Railway Modelling Right Track No 7: Building Buildings, Geoff Taylor (Activity Media)

1 Location

The fundamental question asked by any railway engineer since the 1860s – and one that the modeller should address before deciding on style, shape or size – is where to put a signalbox. If modelling was simply a case of copying the real world there would be no problem, but with so much compression required, even for fictitious locations, siting a model signalbox in a convincing place requires an understanding of what governed the situation of the real thing.

Mechanical considerations

Looking at the traditional mechanical signalbox, the very first consideration – a fundamental law of physics that applies to every mechanical installation – is the fact that there is a direct relationship between the distance from the operator and the piece of equipment being operated, and the route that the connection takes. The further away the equipment and the more convoluted the route, the less mechanically efficient the operation becomes, due to loss of power in transmission. It is unlikely that scaling down the distances between signals and signalbox will be a problem, but on the average small layout you could find you have points/turnouts too far away from the signalbox that is supposed to be controlling them, and it will certainly pay to think about the route taken by physical connections between signalbox and equipment.

Authentic distances between signalboxes and signals in mechanical installations can be gleaned from signalbox diagrams and notices of signalling alterations, which all railway companies issued regularly to operating staff [**4**]. The positioning of turnouts on running lines was regulated from the middle of the 19th century by the Board of Trade, distances appearing in published 'requirements' for new lines, issued periodically between 1858 and the end of World War 1 (when the Ministry of Transport took over the Board's responsibilities).

The signal that was usually the furthest from the signalbox operating it was the distant signal. Prior to the 1880s the regulations governing the way this signal was operated varied between companies, but from that decade, when the basic principles of block working were standardised, the role of the distant signal was to give drivers advance warning of the indication of the next stop signal. It was, therefore, important that the distant signal should be positioned so that once its indication was visible to the locomotive crew, a train could be brought to a stand at the next stop signal. On rising gradients the distance between distant and home signal might be as little as 500yd (457m), but on falling gradients, or where train speeds were high, the signal might be almost a mile (1,760yd or 1,609m) away. By the 1870s the GNR, with its reputation for fast trains, had distant signals up to 1,290yd (1,180m) from home signals on the main line between Grantham and Peterborough. At the beginning of the 20th century on the LNWR distant signals were usually between 1,400yd and 1,700yd (1,280m and 1,550m) from the signalbox, some of those at or beyond this limit being worked by the pulling of two levers in the signalbox (the first to take the slack out of the wire). An extreme example was the use of three levers to work Duston West Junction's down distant, 1 mile 140yd (1,737m) from the signalbox! Other examples from other companies could be given, but these are sufficient, as this is a book about signalboxes not the positioning of signals.

Perhaps of more relevance to the modeller are the distances between signalboxes and the points/turnouts they work mechanically. The Board of Trade first laid down a maximum distance between signalbox and mechanically worked facing points used by passenger trains in its 1874 'requirements'. This was 120yd (110m) – 1,440mm in 4mm scale. By the time a new edition of the 'requirements' was published in 1900 the distance had been eased to 200yd (183m) – 2,400mm in 4mm scale. The intervening period witnessed the construction of most of the country's traditional mechanical signalboxes, so (unless you are modelling a completely non-prototypical scene or something more accurate but with a post-1900 structure) the positioning of your signalbox will have to take these distances into account. For example, if you are modelling a single-track branch line as it might have appeared in this period, with a station crossing loop 300yd (274m) in length (either the scale equivalent or taking modelling compression into account), two signalboxes will be required at either end of that loop. If you are modelling the same station after 1925, when the permitted distance for mechanically worked facing points had increased to 350yd (320m), you will need only one signalbox. Of course, if you are really keen you could model three signalboxes – two from the 1874-1900 period, still in use, whilst their replacement nears completion. Such would have been the case at Bridgnorth in 1923, for example, when the north and south signalboxes were replaced by one on the station platform [**5, 6**].

At the end of the 19th century, when reliable means were perfected for working points/turnouts other than by direct mechanical connections from the signalbox (e.g. pneumatically or electrically) and where these power sources were installed, the Board of Trade distances for mechanically operated facing points did not apply.

4

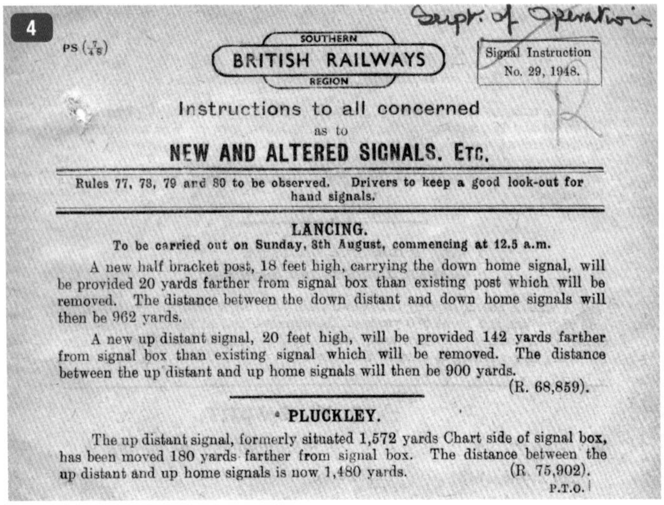

PS (7/48)

SOUTHERN BRITISH RAILWAYS REGION

Signal Instruction No. 29, 1948.

Supt. of Operation

Instructions to all concerned as to

NEW AND ALTERED SIGNALS, ETC.

Rules 77, 78, 79 and 80 to be observed. Drivers to keep a good look-out for hand signals.

LANCING.

To be carried out on Sunday, 8th August, commencing at 12.5 a.m.

A new half bracket post, 18 feet high, carrying the down home signal, will be provided 20 yards farther from signal box than existing post which will be removed. The distance between the down distant and down home signals will then be 962 yards.

A new up distant signal, 20 feet high, will be provided 142 yards farther from signal box than existing signal which will be removed. The distance between the up distant and up home signals will then be 900 yards.

(R. 68,859).

PLUCKLEY.

The up distant signal, formerly situated 1,572 yards Chart side of signal box, has been moved 180 yards farther from signal box. The distance between the up distant and up home signals is now 1,480 yards. (R. 75,902).

P.T.O.

LEFT Alteration of Signals notice issued in the summer of 1948 to inform staff that the distant signals at Lancing and Pluckley were being repositioned. *Author's collection*

RIGHT With the passing of the Regulation of Railways Act in 1889 the Great Western Railway was obliged to interlock its track layout at Bridgnorth, and because contemporary Board of Trade 'requirements' stipulated that facing points should be no further than 180yd (164.6m) from a signalbox the company had to provide two. The signalboxes opened in 1892, and this photograph shows that at the south end of the station. Barely 10 years later the maximum distance for facing points was increased to 250yd (228.6m), enabling the GWR to replace both signalboxes with just one – on the station platform – in 1923.
Author's collection

Line of sight

You may feel these scale distances for distant signals and facing points are unlikely to influence where you position your model signalbox, but the following considerations most certainly should.

Of all railway buildings the signalbox was the only structure erected predominantly as an observation platform. Until well into the 20th century it was considered very important that the signalman should be able to see everything under his control and not have to rely on mechanical or electrical devices indicating whether or not a piece of equipment had responded correctly to the operation of a lever. There were two basic schools of thought as to how best to achieve a clear view. The first was to position the signalbox close to the track or with the operating room elevated no higher than the loading gauge. The advantage of this was that the signalman could closely observe passing trains, communicate easily with train crew and react quickly if there were a problem. The second choice was to erect tall structures [**7**] or position signalboxes on top of embankments away from the track so that the signalman could see as far as possible and anticipate the approach of trains. All pre-Grouping railway companies built signalboxes in both these categories, although the consideration of height had been most important before the block system was adopted. By the time C. B. Byles, Signal Engineer of the LYR, published his book *The First Principles of Railway Signalling* in 1910, when the block system was fully developed and electrical devices 'repeating' the indications of signals and points not visible to the signalman were accepted as reliable equipment, he was able to comment that the building of tall structures was no longer necessary and that '... the continued erection of abnormally high 'boxes on some railways is probably due to traditional usage' [**8**].

LEFT Standing in the 1923 signalbox at Bridgnorth, the signalman poses for the camera as '43xx' 2-6-0 No 6388 trundles through with empties from Buildwas Power Station to Highley in the early 1960s.
S. K. Blencowe collection

7
KIRTON LIME SIDINGS

LEFT The operating room of the MSLR signalbox at Kirton Lime Sidings is level with the adjacent road, enabling the signalman to see over the bridge from which this photograph was taken in May 2010. The 'box provides another example of weatherboarding. *Author*

8

If you are going to model a signalbox close to the track it is important to imagine yourself down by the lineside, viewing the scene as though you were the signal engineer or member of the siting committee deliberating on-site. In 4mm scale you will be about 20mm above track level, trying to calculate what the elevation of your new signalbox should be. Always try and imagine what the view would be from the operating floor of your signalbox [**9**]. Would your signalman be able to see his distant signals (if that curve imposed on you by restricted modelling space was not there)? Is there an over bridge, or platform canopy, water tower or warehouse or perhaps a tree obstructing the signalman's view? Are all your facing points clearly visible from the signalbox? If not, the Board of Trade inspector would be unlikely to grant you permission to run trains. Will trains frequently stand or shunt in front of your signalbox, obscuring the view of other lines? If your signalbox is at a terminus, near a locomotive depot or marshalling yard, would drifting smoke from all those standing or shunting locomotives make the signalman's job more difficult? Remember that smog and thick fogs were genuine problems for the Victorians, and railway companies had special rules for such conditions.

If your signalman is controlling a level crossing, make sure he can see approaching road traffic before operating the gates. When the crossing keeper at the GNR's level crossing at High Street, Lincoln, was dispensed with, and the gates were worked electrically from

9

ABOVE The three-flight timber staircase emphasises the height of the GNSR signalbox at Dyce, photographed in 1937. Note too the subtle details in the overall design: the stone 'plinth' on which sits the operating floor, the slight 'pagoda-style' flaring of the roof, the offset pattern of slates and the generous finials. *Ian Allan Library*

LEFT When this photograph was taken in 1978 there was still a clear view through the tunnel from the SER's Salisbury Tunnel Junction signalbox. Again, the details are worth noting: the three-plank bench, probably as old as the signalbox (1860s), the hand-painted lever-description plates, fitted sometime between 1923 and 1948, and the 'modern' two-bar heater. *Author's collection*

LEFT Photographed in a flurry of Christmas snow in 1996, the extension to the GNR High Street signalbox at Lincoln is very obvious. It was built in 1925 when the electrically powered crossing gates were installed. Note the careful matching of the brickwork and the style of locking-room window, even though the signalbox was almost 50 years old when this was done. *Author*

BELOW As there was barely 12ft (3.6m) of available space between the down loop and the boundary with adjacent farmland the MR was obliged to erect this structure in 1900 at what it named Kilby Bridge, a few miles south of Leicester. This interesting signalbox is now preserved at Hammersmith, the western extremity of the Midland Railway Centre's line through Butterley. *Author*

the adjacent signalbox, that structure was provided with a narrow extension from where the signalman could see the road whilst operating the new equipment [**10**].

If you opt for a tall signalbox, make sure there are good reasons to justify why your railway company was prepared to go to the expense of using extra timber, bricks or stonework. Do you really need such a tall signalbox in the middle of the Fens or Chat Moss? Are you about to build a signalbox with a tall stone lower storey on an embankment that could not possibly support such a structure? Have you provided your signalman with a wonderful view over that road bridge only to discover that his view of the platform starting signals and the crossover road is obscured by those canopies on the station platform?

Whether or not you provide an elevated signalbox will also depend on the railway company you are using as inspiration. Some pre-Grouping companies were more reluctant than others to build tall structures. The MR achieved greater standardisation in signalbox design than did any other pre-Grouping company and tried to avoid building special structures. However, if there was restricted space at the lineside, it, like other companies, was forced to build (or have built for it) signalboxes with a narrow locking room or lower storey [**11**], cantilevered out from the sides of cuttings or, in extreme cases, positioned on wrought-iron or steel frameworks over the running lines. Most pre-Grouping companies had examples of all these forms of special signalbox, and some were very impressive structures. The signalbox suspended over the lines at the LSWR's London terminus of Waterloo, for example, was the largest of its type and had two mechanical lever frames with a total of 262 levers when it was replaced by a new installation with miniature levers in 1936.

ABOVE Canterbury West was opened by the SR in 1928. If you ignore the metal bridge, it is essentially a standard signalbox, only its means of elevation and its orientation to the tracks making it appear unusual. *Author*

RIGHT The signalbox provided by the LYR at its Wigan (Wallgate) station was, like Canterbury West, another standard structure raised up on an open metal frame. Using the L&Y Society's classification, this signalbox was a size 10, officially 34ft 3¼in (10.4m) in length, so that it could accommodate a mechanical frame of 55 levers. *W. Potter*

ABOVE Huddersfield No 1 signalbox was a good example of an LNWR overhead structure, lacking a locking room (which the 'boxes at Canterbury and Wigan retained) because the company had developed a variation of its standard interlocking that could be fixed immediately behind the levers. (Don't you get the feeling that access to the operating room was through that open window?)
Roger Carpenter collection

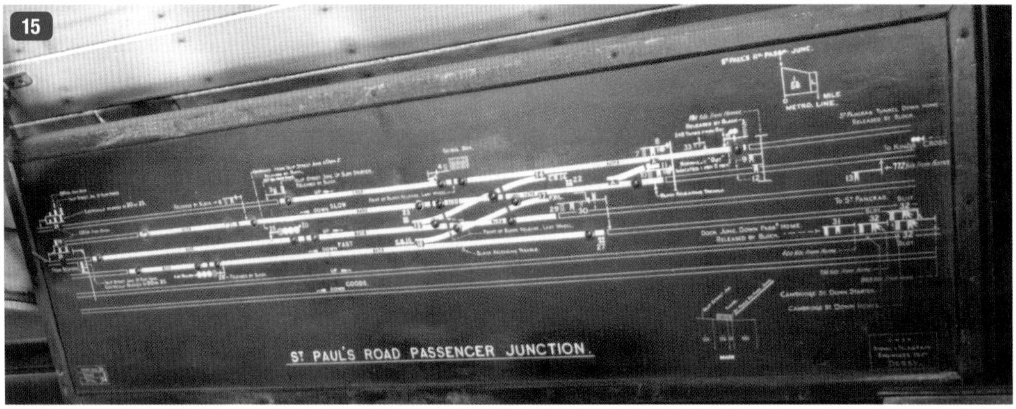

ABOVE The illuminated track diagram, added by the LMS, inside the MR signalbox at St Paul's Road Passenger Junction, just outside St Pancras station.
Author's collection

The design of the LSWR's Waterloo signalbox was unique and as such will perhaps be of limited inspirational use to the majority of modellers. Other 'overhead' structures might be of more interest, however. Some of these were full-size signalboxes simply perched on a metal lattice [**12, 13**], whilst those of the LNWR, for example, were cut-down versions of its standard signalbox design, possible because the company had developed a particular form of interlocking that could be positioned immediately behind the lever frame, thus eliminating the need for the lower storey – the 'locking' room [**14**].

The type of control equipment inside other railways' overhead signalboxes also affected their design. When the NER resignalled Newcastle station and its approaches in the first decade of the 20th century it was able to build signalboxes smaller than would have been necessary to house traditional mechanical lever frames because it used electro-pneumatic equipment activated by miniature levers, with all the associated interlocking, switch-gear, etc incorporated into the same metal frame bolted to the operating floor. The LSWR benefited in the same way when, between 1907 and 1912, it erected

a number of new overhead signalboxes equipped with low-pressure pneumatic equipment on the lines between Vauxhall and Clapham Junction.

ABOVE The archetypal powerbox of its era, Broxbourne was opened in 1960. The overhanging canopy, attached to the roof to shade the operating room from direct sunlight, shows up well in this photograph. *BR(ER)*

Out of sight

The development of new control equipment, in which the direct mechanical link between signalbox and lineside equipment was removed, laid the foundations for modern signalling. Equipment could be located further from the signalbox but was then more likely to be out of sight, and this meant that electrical indicators back in the signalbox were vital to tell signalmen whether or not equipment had operated correctly (see Chapter 4). After World War 1 confidence in electrical 'repeaters' increased, and from early experiments in the first decade of the 20th century with the use of discrete track circuits to tell a signalman whether or not a train was occupying a particular stretch of track, the march of technology had by the 1930s given birth to the illuminated track diagram [**15**]. By the end of that decade the North Eastern Area of the LNER was convinced of the reliability of electrically worked signals, points and track circuiting and completed a number of innovative signalling installations. The largest, albeit completed after nationalisation, was at York. Here for the first time a major railway centre was controlled by signalmen who could not see any of the signals or points they controlled, nor any of the trains passing their workplace. The signalbox was more akin to a large open-plan office, and one can only wonder as to the thoughts of the signalmen, all of whom had worked hitherto in the sometimes noisy and always physically demanding mechanical NER signalboxes in and around the city.

Given that track circuiting became the cornerstone of all progressive resignalling work, it is surprising that as signalboxes evolved into powerboxes in the 1960s [**16**] and finally into signalling centres in the 1980s, these were still built next to the lineside and with windows (albeit often small) overlooking the track. Logically, if the area under the control of a signalbox was fully track-circuited, with colour-light signals and electrically worked points, level crossings monitored by CCTV and train crews able to communicate with signalmen from lineside telephones, the signalbox could be located anywhere, with no necessity for signalmen to see any trains at all during their shifts. Even after the introduction, starting with Liverpool Street in 1989, of the Integrated Electronic Control Centre (IECC), some of which were located some distance from the lineside, the majority of signalboxes old and new remained adjacent to all or some parts of the tracks they controlled.

Getting to work

Concluding this chapter on where your signalbox, powerbox or signalling centre should be located is one last but very important consideration which once again requires you to shrink yourself to the scale you are modelling and attempt to walk about on the layout you have created. Can the model signalman or signalwoman reach his or her place of work? Unless you are assuming that he/she will walk along the track, that path to the signalbox from the nearest public road or farmer's track can add a final touch of realism to the location of your signalbox.

2 Size and materials

It might seem an obvious point to make, but the size of all mechanical signalboxes, powerboxes and ultimately (to a certain extent) signalling centres is determined largely by the amount of equipment inside. It would have been pointless and unjustifiably expensive to build a structure larger than absolutely necessary to perform its intended function. Architectural style has played a part in the look of signalboxes since the 1870s (*see* Chapter 3), but it has rarely influenced their size [17].

The main reason for making this point is that the more realistic you wish your model railway to be, the more important it is to try and think yourself inside the heads of railway managers, board members, engineers and any other people who, in real life, would have had a say in why something was built, where it was built, what it looked like, how efficient it was relevant to its function and, more importantly, how the initial cost compared with its revenue-earning potential. Railways did not build things merely to look good. They did build things to impress shareholders and the public, but this was fundamentally to boost or bolster trade and/or to inspire confidence, because everything in which they invested had to make money for the company (even if, at certain times in the history of Britain's railways, this was little more than a theoretical exercise).

As most model signalboxes are purely decorative and contain no working equipment, there is physically nothing to determine the size of structure you choose apart from a desire to be as historically correct as possible. Physically there is nothing to stop you providing a 250-lever-frame, 50ft-tall, all-stone signalbox at your wooden platform halt on a single-track branch line with no signals or points/turnouts. You might become a talking-point amongst other modellers if you did, but you have that freedom. You can be lavish if you want to, because there is no model financial director and no tiny shareholders to please, (although there may be other real-life financial and family constraints). Be that as it may, the following are some useful observations about the real thing that might help you decide the size and proportions of your model signalbox.

Proportions

The basic rule with traditional mechanical signalboxes is that in the majority of structures, regardless of height, the lower storey or locking room will be of the same dimensions in plan as the upper storey – the operating room, where the signalman works. If the site for the signalbox was restricted the locking room might be smaller in plan with the upper storey oversailing **[18]** or, in some overhead signalboxes, non-existent, as outlined in the previous chapter.

When signalboxes were built to house other than mechanical lever frames, the relative sizes of the operating room and locking room could vary. In the 1930s, the LNER made the first significant break with tradition when it built new signalboxes to house panels of switches and buttons to operate signals and points at Thirsk (1933), Leeds (1937), Hull Paragon (1938) **[19]** and finally at Northallerton (1939). In these buildings, although the width (or depth) was the same, the length (parallel with the track) of the operating room was much less than that of the lower locking room, containing the necessary electrical relays. A practical response to what was needed, the new configuration turned out to be aesthetically pleasing, and the form was developed in a more architecturally bold way by the SR for its new 'Glasshouse'- or 'Queen Mary'-style structures of the same period, Surbiton, opened in 1936, being the first. The SR obviously liked the effect of the operating floor perched on a longer locking room, which evoked the shape of an ocean liner, and although it was not strictly necessary for the signalling

17

LEFT Newton Abbot East signalbox, looking a little shabby but still impressive just two years before closure, in 1987. It was built by the GWR in 1928 to house a frame of 206 levers. *Author*

RIGHT Templecombe signalbox, photographed in 1988, by which time it was almost exactly 50 years old. *J. C. Hillmer*

19

LEFT Hull Paragon signalbox was still a handsome building when photographed in 1996. Note the alternating bands of projecting stretcher bond brickwork; also the later bricking-up of the locking-room windows, which has had the unintentional effect of brightening its appearance. *Author*

BELOW Mostyn signalbox, built by the LNWR in 1902 in a restricted space between the running lines. *Author*

18

equipment they had to house the company erected a number of such buildings with mechanical lever frames (at Horsham, Bognor Regis and Templecombe in 1938, for example [**20**]), taking advantage of the longer lower storey to incorporate rooms for purposes other than signalling.

Size

For a brief period in the 1860s influential signalling engineer John Saxby supplied signalboxes that were square in plan. This was partly because the structures usually contained fewer levers than in later periods, but it may have also been a form of standardisation, given that most of his signalboxes of this period were constructed of prefabricated wooden panels. His firm – Saxby & Farmer – also erected brick-built signalboxes that were almost square in plan, and it is obvious that other companies were influenced by the proportions of these structures when they came to erect their own signalboxes [**21**].

However, during the 1870s signalboxes that were rectangular in plan began to predominate, the longest horizontal dimension being determined by the length of the lever frame. Length is probably the most crucial dimension to try and get right in model form, as it has a direct relationship with the track layout. Broadly speaking, the number of levers reflects the number of signals and points/turnouts in your track layout. As the length of a frame was also determined

20

by the spacing between levers (the pitch), and this varied between railway companies and signalling contractors, all these considerations are examined in detail in Chapter 4. Although the length of mechanical signalboxes varied, their width became surprisingly standardised throughout the country, varying between 10ft (3m) and 12ft (3.6m).

The height of mechanical signalboxes could vary depending on their location (as examined in Chapter 1), but for the majority of railway companies the height of the operating floor above track level, when line of sight was not an issue, was usually about 8ft (2.4m).

Signalboxes built by railway companies and signalling contractors from prefabricated wooden panels were generally more standardised than was the case with brick- or stone-built structures. The MR provides a very good example of what could be achieved. Between 1870 and 1923 the company used the same basic design for the majority of its 1,500 signalboxes. In that period Derby Signal Works turned out panels in just four standard widths – 10ft (3m), 12ft (3.6m), 12ft 10in (3.9m) and 15ft (4.5m) [**22**, **23**, **24**, **25**, **26**]. This degree of standardisation was possible because the MR also produced its own lever frames made up of standard-size single lever units, whole frames invariably made up of multiples of four levers, i.e. 12, 16, 20, 24, etc. (*see* Chapter 4.)

21

LEFT Marsh Brook signalbox, on the Shrewsbury–Hereford line, photographed in spring 1986, before this view was obscured. The 1872 structure was almost a clone of John Saxby's first signalboxes. Having just been repointed, the Flemish bond brickwork shows up here to advantage. Notice the generous stock of coal to the left. *Author*

As more signalboxes with electronic panels began to appear in the 1950s what might be termed the 1930s art-deco proportions mentioned above were increasingly adopted [**27**]. Even if the size of the 'locking' room remained constant, as would have been the case if mechanical interlocking had been used in the same location, the operating room could be so much smaller, having to accommodate a panel a fraction the size of the equivalent lever frame.

When the first generation of powerboxes followed in the 1960s, controlling much larger areas, the operating room did begin to increase in size, often having to accommodate an arc of panels as well as traffic controllers with desks and telephones. But it was the lower storeys that grew most conspicuously, having to house many more relays. So as not to make these inconveniently long, the whole building was often increased in height, so that by the 1970s many powerboxes were huge slabs of buildings, almost tower blocks [**28**], incorporating rooms for a variety of uses and far removed from their Victorian signalbox predecessors.

Miniaturisation and computer technology finally cut powerboxes down to size in the 1980s, when they were transformed into signalling centres and, with a move away from the 'brutalist' style of architecture, became either completely anonymous warehouse-type structures or post-modern, architect-designed buildings.

In the recent past, large-scale resignalling projects have given way to more modest replacement schemes in which either existing signalboxes have been modified for their new use or completely new structures closer to the size of the average mechanical signalbox have been erected, their style often having 'heritage' overtones [**29**].

Extensions

Extending mechanical signalboxes rather than building completely new structures was obviously considered cost-effective throughout the Victorian era and through to the 1940s, as there were so many examples [**30**]. Such modification usually involved increasing the length of the original structure, sometimes the width and occasionally the height.

The fact that most extensions maintained the architectural integrity of the original building attests to the pride companies had in their buildings. It has always surprised the author that a signalbox that was probably architecturally 'old-fashioned' and built of materials no longer available at the time of its extension was (usually) modified with such care. There were examples of ham-fisted extensions, of course, but not that many.

When wooden signalboxes were enlarged it was comparatively easy to blend in the extension with the original structure, but with masonry it could be more difficult. This was especially the case when bricks of the size used in the original construction were no longer available and a different 'standard' had to be used [**31**, **32**, **33**].

If the signalbox was already in a restricted space and an extension was needed, some constructional ingenuity was required. Extending the locking room might involve narrowing one end or building one of the walls at an angle to avoid existing trackwork. This might result in the operating floor overhanging at that end, as it was not usually practical to provide a narrower extension to this space [**34**].

The job of extending signalboxes would have caused a lot of disruption for signalmen. It must have been difficult to cope with the removal of a wall and the subsequent loss of heat in exchange for fresh air and brick, mortar and sawdust. And that was before S&T staff got fiddling with the lever frame. Here, then, is a real modelling opportunity – that of re-creating a signalbox during just such an alteration, with the end wall missing, giving you the chance to show off that detailed interior. (*see* Chapter 4 for inspiration.)

Other alterations

Protecting signalboxes from bomb and shrapnel damage in strategic locations all over the country during World War 2 altered the size and appearance of many structures. Building a brick skin around the lower storey was a common modification at strategic railway centres, sometimes increasing the width considerably when walls were made thick enough to withstand a major impact. Where a signalbox already had brick- or stone-built lower storeys, locking-room windows were often bricked up and in most cases never unblocked after the end of hostilities. At Salisbury the pitched timber roofs of the two ex-LSWR signalboxes containing pneumatic equipment were replaced by flat concrete roofs [**35**].

Reductions rather than extensions also affected the size and proportions of some signalboxes. Alterations in this category were more likely to be repairs forced on a railway by factors beyond its control. Pitched roofs damaged by fire were sometimes replaced by cheaper flat examples [**36**]. The construction of a new road bridge in the 1970s obliged British Rail to remove the pitched roof from the very long York Yard North signalbox (at one time housing 150 levers) and substitute a flat one.

Material choices

Once you have decided upon the size and proportions of your model signalbox, the next consideration concerns the materials to be portrayed.

In the real world the choice of materials (and often the style) depended partly on the way in which a railway company's signalbox design had evolved from its signalling-hut predecessors. (Compare the photographs of the NBR's signal hut at Belses and the same company's fully fledged signalbox at Jedburgh [see **2**, **78**]). As might be imagined, most huts have traditionally been constructed of timber – a material easy to work, cheaper than masonry and, although not

LEFT One 10ft panel in length: Cottage Lane Crossing signalbox, on the line between Newark and Lincoln. Although this structure was erected in 1928 and acquired a brick base much later it had a pure MR pedigree. Note too the corrugated-tin lamp room to the left. *Author*

BELOW Two 10ft panels in length: Sileby signalbox, opened on the main line between Trent and Leicester in 1898 and closed in 1987. *Author*

ABOVE One 15ft panel in length: the former Ais Gill signalbox, now masquerading as Butterley Ground Frame at the Midland Railway Centre. The signalbox was opened in 1900 and remained in main-line service for just over 80 years. *Author*

RIGHT Three 10ft panels in length: Syston North Junction, also between Trent and Leicester, opened in 1891 and closed at the same time as Sileby. *Author*

26

LEFT One 12ft panel in width; unfortunately this postcard did not record the location of the MR signalbox. *Author's collection*

expected to have the same lifespan, easier to repair. At first, wooden huts for signalling purposes were erected only to provide shelter for railway policemen, pointsmen and signalmen – and, for a small number of progressive railways, to house any electrical devices that might be employed for communicating between huts. Pre-1860s mechanical equipment was invariably not given any shelter. Small huts of wooden construction with mechanical equipment in the open air reflected the relative importance placed by companies on train control.

As regulations tightened and traffic increased during the 1870s, requiring more equipment to control the movement of trains at and between stations, many railway companies preferred to build signalboxes in brick or stone. Mechanical lever frames and electrical instruments for block working represented big investments for cost-conscious Victorian railway companies (albeit not always willingly embraced), so the structures housing those assets needed to provide them with adequate protection. But brick never completely replaced timber as a building material for signalboxes. Interestingly, after 10-15 years of building signalboxes with brick locking rooms the GNR turned to all-timber construction in the 1880s, when it became apparent that some of those first generation of signalboxes were not going to be the permanent structures envisaged when they were built and that, as result of modification and expansion of track layouts, some would have comparatively short lives [**37**, **38**].

Timber

As outlined earlier, John Saxby set the standard for the archetypal signalbox with his timber structures of the 1860s, taking as his model the telegraph towers of the late 18th and early 19th centuries, and from then until the 1970s mechanical signalboxes made up of prefabricated wood panels could be found all over the country [**39**].

There was nothing unusual about the constructional details or the method of erecting wooden signalboxes. A box frame of stout vertical, horizontal and diagonal timbers was clad with either vertical or horizontal boards, or for effect, with boards laid down at 45° [see **66**]. On some mid-19th century signalboxes the cladding was attached to the inside of the building so as to expose the frame, but, as there were then many places where rainwater could collect and cause rot, this design feature fell out of favour [**40**]. All of the first generation of standard signalboxes built by the LSWR in the 1870s with exposed frames were later clad with horizontal or vertical boarding [*see* **61**].

The style of cladding also conformed to established standards of joinery and if reproduced correctly will enhance the appearance of any model. (The various styles are described in the photograph captions.) All exposed timber in a signalbox, inside and out, was painted. No stripped pine for the Victorians!

Access to the operating room of the majority of signalboxes, of whatever construction, was via external steps formed of parallel boards with timber treads and no risers. However, some brick- and stone-built structures were graced with stone steps, and from the late 1930s a number of designs incorporated a brick or concrete staircase as part of the structure [see **43**]. Within the last two decades, where external staircases cannot be avoided, a new generation of Health & Safety-conscious managers have insisted on replacing timber with welded, galvanised-steel fabrications [*see* **81**].

Before concluding this section it is appropriate to mention roof construction and cladding, as the majority of signalboxes, regardless of what the walls were made of, had timber-framed roofs. Until the 1930s all signalboxes had pitched roofs like any other permanent building. On Saxby's first structures these were of the hipped form, i.e. all four faces of the roof sloped. The form that became most common and lent itself to simpler extensions if the structure needed to be elongated was the gabled roof. In this form the two end walls were taken up to the ridge line of the roof (i.e. its highest point), with only two faces of the roof sloping (usually those parallel to the track). Both these basic roof forms could be – and were – modified for architectural effect, but, naturally, most railway companies did not feel the extra expense was justified [*see* **8**, **69**].

From a modeller's point of view it does not really matter what material was used for the framework of the roof, but getting the cladding right is important. Sheets of zinc laid on roofs with very shallow pitches were used on small signalboxes of the 1860s. Corrugated iron was favoured by the Highland Railway [*see* **60**] and also appeared on signalboxes supplied by signalling contractor Dutton for the Cambrian Railways at the end of the 19th century. Asbestos tiles were used on concrete signalboxes built between the two world wars by the GWR [*see* **42**]. Surprisingly, given how common they were on

ABOVE The Eastern Region of British Railways continued the pioneering work of the LNER after World War 2 with the electrification and resignalling of the lines between London's Liverpool Street station and Shenfield, completed in the spring of 1949. The architecture of this signalbox at Goodmayes was deliberately 'modern' to create a complete break with the past. *BR(ER)*

RIGHT The powerbox at Birmingham New Street station, photographed when brand-new in 1966. *Kidderminster Railway Museum/ Westinghouse Archive*

RIGHT Whereas Goodmayes projected the confident face of change, Allington Junction signalbox, constructed 56 years later, in 2005, to replace the GNR signalbox [see 57] reflects a less confident age. It has clean contemporary lines but an old-fashioned pitched roof and, compared with the uncompromisingly 'modern' Sleaford South signalbox of 1957 [98], has a somewhat self-effacing feel. *Author*

BELOW Only the two bricked-up locking-room windows betray the fact that Harlescott signalbox, north of Shrewsbury on the line to Crewe, has more than doubled in size since it was erected by the LNWR in 1882. *Author*

ABOVE An Edwardian photograph of the 1874 signalbox built by the GNR at Carlton-on-Trent station, on the main line between Retford and Newark. *Author's collection*

domestic houses in almost every part of the country, clay roofing tiles were never as popular as standard Welsh slates, and from the 1870s slates became the preferred choice for almost every traditional mechanical signalbox. The most common size was 20in (510mm) x 10in (255mm), and they were laid, as is still the normal practice today, in horizontal, overlapping rows to create a pattern of offset squares.

After World War 2, in line with contemporary architectural practice, most new signalboxes were built with flat roofs [**41**]. This trend continued until the 1980s, when the pitched roofs made a return, the most incongruous example of this renaissance being their addition to the 1960s powerboxes at Trent and Derby.

Masonry

We return now to the walls of signalboxes, which over the years have been built variously of brick, stone and concrete. It is probably fair to state that the Victorian era was a golden age for construction in brick and stone. During this period the combined skills of architect,

32

ABOVE A photograph taken a century later in 1976 from almost the same position. Because the whole of the end gable including the decorative barge board and the toilet hut are the same, at first sight it is difficult to tell the signalbox has been extended. The three original end window casements were used on the front extension with new, but matching, fixed casements made for the end. *Author*

33

ABOVE The extension was more obvious on the front. Both the original and new brickwork were laid in English bond, but because the brick sizes were different no attempt was made to tie in the new with the old. This photograph was taken in 1977 shortly after closure and immediately prior to demolition. *Author*

engineer and artisan led to the erection of the country's finest brick- and stone-built structures. Although signalboxes were simple affairs in comparison with civic buildings, warehouses, endless rows of terraced housing, viaducts and the London sewers, the same quality of workmanship was usually apparent.

As was the case with timber, constructing signalboxes in brick or stone required exactly the same skills as were employed throughout the building industry. The thickness of walls depended on their height and the load of any floors they had to support. The way in which bricks or stones were laid together – their coursing – conformed to contemporary standards. With bricks, both strength and beauty was achieved using a variety of different 'bonds', an art that has largely died out. (The most common brick bonds used in signalbox construction are described in the photograph captions.) In the days of lime mortar the joints between bricks were tight – as little as 3mm on the very best facework. The same held true for the best stonework. From the 1950s, however, the almost universal use of stretcher bond combined with cement mortar increased the gap between bricks, and today the vast majority of bricks (other than specials) are proportioned so as to maintain a gap of no less than 10mm and often more, as the British Standard tolerance for bricks is so generous.

Not everyone is a fan of brick, like this author, so incorrect brickwork is unlikely to prompt as much comment as modelling a concrete signalbox. At the end of the first decade of the 20th century William Marriot of the MGNJR experimented with reinforced concrete, casting everything from signal posts to building blocks. Scarcity of steel and, particularly, good-quality timber for railway work during and after World War 1 helped promote its use, and in the 1920s hundreds of reinforced concrete signal posts were erected all over the country. Concrete blocks for buildings, however, did not become as popular, and only a few signalboxes were constructed of this material. According to the research done by the Signalling Study Group in the 1970s and '80s, between 1927 and 1933 the GWR erected 20 signalboxes with steel, load-bearing frames that were then filled with concrete blocks. This was not a tentative experiment by the company; some of these signalboxes were large buildings, Didcot East Junction, for example, housing a frame of 150 levers **[42]** However, in sharp contrast to the faith shown in what at the time was still an unusual building material and which represented a radical departure for the company, the proportions of all the new signalboxes conformed to contemporary GWR standard signalbox design, right down to the distinctive pattern of glass panes in the window casements.

In the 1930s concrete sills and lintels were often used instead of timber or brick arches in new but traditional brick-built signalboxes constructed by all of the 'Big Four' companies. In some, concrete was also used decoratively to create horizontal bands of rendering, and in the new SR 'Glasshouse'-style structures it was cast to form the name of the signalbox.

During World War 2 and thereafter until the 1970s concrete was more likely to be used in roof construction. Flat, reinforced concrete roofs had been purely an architectural feature of the SR's 'Glasshouse' signalboxes of the 1930s, but in wartime they were viewed as a practical protection for signalmen during air raids. There were obvious advantages and disadvantages of working under a thick reinforced slab of concrete at such times, but arguments for the former must have prevailed, because all companies, responding to 'ARP' (Air Raid Precaution) recommendations, developed signalbox designs with this feature **[43]**.

The final materials to be mentioned in regard to signalbox construction and modification are pressed steel and PVC. The former has found limited use **[44]**, but replacement window frames fabricated from the latter have changed – indeed, are continuing to change – the character of many of the last surviving traditional mechanical signalboxes. (*see* Chapter 3.)

34

35

ABOVE Quite inexplicably impressive buildings resulted from the fitting of flat concrete roofs to both Salisbury East and West signalboxes during World War 2. The English bond brickwork in the blocked-up locking room windows was neatly done, obviously with some pride. BR(SR)

ABOVE Despite the overhead clutter it is still very obvious that although the operating and locking rooms both taper, the roof of Stockport No 1 signalbox remains defiantly rectangular in plan. (Note too the late-20th-century Health & Safety fire escape, leading not to firm ground but to the point rodding.) *Author*

RIGHT The flat roof added in January 1984 to the MR signalbox at Kibworth, on the main line between Leicester and Bedford, kept the signalbox operational for another two years and five months, until it was declared redundant. This photograph is useful inasmuch as it shows the height of the panelling immediately above the windows, which in almost all other photographs is obscured by the roof overhang. *Author*

36

37

38

ABOVE This interesting Edwardian photograph shows the first brick-built signalbox at Letchworth, erected by the GNR in 1874. The decorative barge-board was a feature favoured by the company at a number of locations during this period [see also 93]. Notice the arched tops to the window casements, adding to the 'Gothic Revival' feel of the architecture. *Author's collection*

LEFT A few years later the local photographer has gone out to record the new all-timber signalbox built by the GNR in 1913 to control the new Garden City station at Letchworth. The structure was perched out on the very edge of the embankment in anticipation of future track expansion. The timber cladding is made up of lapped boards. *Author's collection*

BELOW The GER signalbox at North Walsham (Type 7 under the Signalling Study Group's classification), photographed in June 1996. A new coat of paint serves to emphasise the simplicity of the structure, consisting of a box frame with weatherboarded panels. *Author*

39

40

41

ABOVE This signalbox, with its exposed timber frame, was the first built by the FR at Silecroft station, at the end of the 1870s, and would be replaced in 1923 by a larger brick-based structure. Note the lack of glazing bars in the windows. *Author's collection*

LEFT A beautifully preserved example of the BR(LMR) Type 15 signalbox at Rawtenstall West, on the East Lancashire Railway. *Author*

RIGHT The uncompromising tin can that is Craven Arms signalbox. The description is appropriate not only on aesthetic grounds, for just as tin cans are containers, this structure was built to enclose the existing GWR timber signalbox. Once the cocoon was finished, in the summer of 2000, various sections of the old timber structure were removed to leave the lever frame. *Author*

42

ABOVE A model signalbox without internal fittings? No; this interesting photograph taken in December 1931 shows Didcot East Junction signalbox as a shell waiting to be fitted out. *D. Wittamore collection/Kidderminster Railway Museum*

RIGHT Wellingborough Junction signalbox, opened in 1943, was an example of the LMS's variety of ARP signalbox, classified LMS Type 13 by the Signalling Study Group. It was photographed in 1984, shortly after closure. *Author*

43

44

3 Style

Although the basic equipment - lever frame and electrical instruments - was the same in every traditional mechanical signalbox, in true British fashion not only did this come in a variety of forms, but from the early 1870s a host of different styles of building began to appear. By the end of the 19th century the style of a signalbox would immediately betray the signalling contractor or railway company that had built it. The construction of signalboxes of distinctive family types for housing either mechanical or electronic control equipment continued until the end of the 1960s, following which powerboxes and signalling centres were erected, each to its own unique design.

Despite obvious preferences, railways (and, later, the regions of British Railways) appear not to have categorised their signalboxes even when they used a variety of different 'standard' designs. The task of creating a classification for signalboxes was taken up in the 1970s and '80s by the Signalling Study Group, and for any modeller serious about the accuracy of his/her model, the results of this group's researches, published by OPC in 1986 as *The Signal Box* (reprinted 1998) are an essential source of reference.

The Signalling Study Group was able fairly readily to categorise signalboxes built prior to the Grouping of 1923, but after that date designs varied more within categories, and for structures built following nationalisation in 1948 the type numbers allocated had to encompass wider variations between individual structures. The one postwar signalbox design that varied the least from the drawing board to the lineside was the BR(LMR) Type 15 [*see* **41**], which perpetuated a level of standardisation in design and execution that had been achieved by one of the LMR's predecessors, the Midland Railway. (A fine model of the brick-based example of this type was produced by Triang in the 1960s.)

Described using the classification system devised by the Signalling Study Group, the following photographs **[45-76]** depict just some of the many types of signalbox built by signalling contractors and railway companies from 1870.

45

ABOVE Dutton Type 1/Highland, Helmsdale (HR). *I. J. Stewart*

46

ABOVE McKenzie & Holland Type 3, Pontrilas (GWR). *Author*

47

LEFT Saxby & Farmer Type 2a, Swindon E (GWR) – a good example of lapped boarding. *F. Moore*

ABOVE Saxby & Farmer Type 5, Warnham (LBSCR). *I. J. Stewart*

LEFT Saxby & Farmer Type 4, Stoke Cannon (GWR). *Author*

BELOW Saxby & Farmer Type 9, Parbold (LYR). *Author*

51

53

ABOVE Railway Signal Co, Elsham (MSLR). *Author*

LEFT CR Type S4, Parklee. *Robert Humm*

BELOW Yardley/Smith Type 1, Whitley Bridge (LYR). *R. S. Carpenter collection*

52

54

55

ABOVE FR Type 1, Bootle. *Author*

LEFT GSWR Type 1, Annan. *I. J. Stewart*

56

57

ABOVE GER Type 3, Acle. *Author*

LEFT GNR Type 1, Allington Junction. *Author*

RIGHT GNSR Type 1, Macduff. *Author's collection*

58

59

60

ABOVE LSWR Type 1, Crediton – a good illustration of weatherboarding above bricks laid in English bond. *Author*

RIGHT LYR, Hebden Bridge. *Author*

LEFT TOP GWR Type 2, Par. *Author*

LEFT BOTTOM HR McKenzie & Holland Type 3/Highland, Dalnaspidal. *H. C. Casserley*

STRAWBERRY HILL JUNCTION

ABOVE LNWR Type 5, Lichfield Trent Valley. On this, the rear elevation of the signalbox, the locking room originally had four recessed panels, which at some point have been bricked in. *Author*

RIGHT MSLR/GCR Type 1, Dovecliffe. *Lens of Sutton collection*

LEFT LSWR Type 4, Strawberry Hill Junction. *Author's collection*

65

66
Stallingborough

LEFT MSLR/GCR Type 2, Stallingborough. All Type 2 signalboxes had timber boarding, the joints between each plank being covered with a batten. *Author*

RIGHT MSLR/GCR Type 5, Neasden South. Note the main distribution telegraph pole, the arms displaying a fine collection of the distinctively shaped Langdon insulator pots. *Author's collection*

67

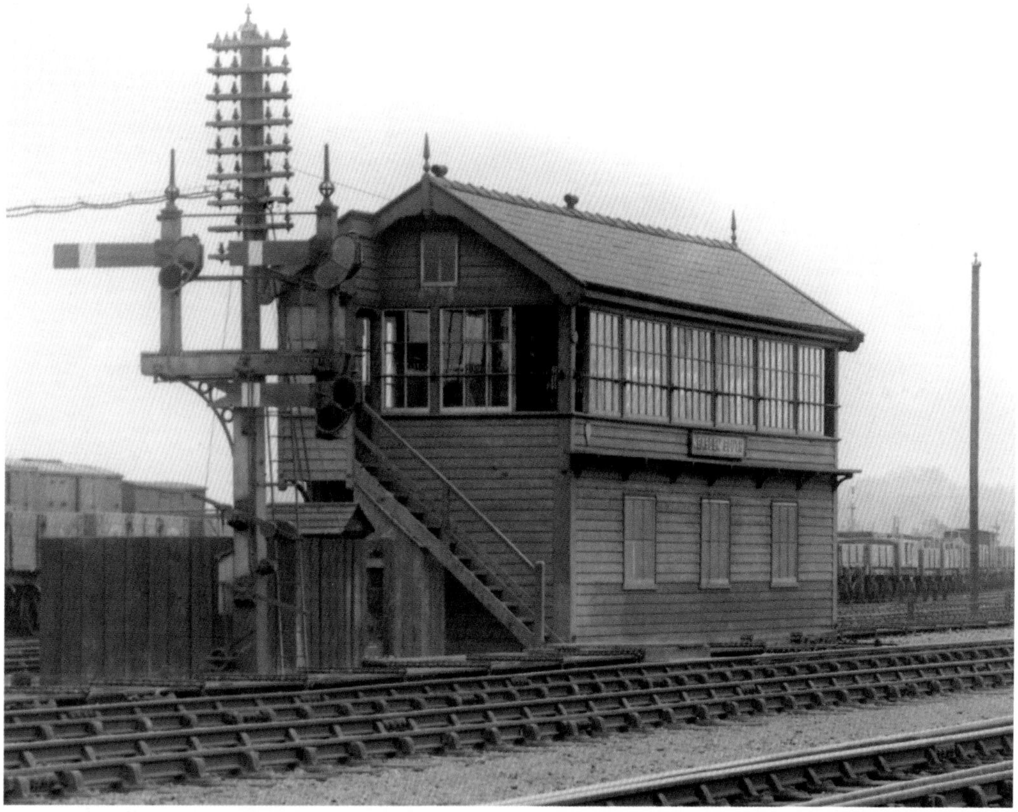

68

LEFT NBR Type 4, Bothwell Junction – another signalbox with a carefully executed extension. *W. A. C. Smith*

69

70

ABOVE NER Type C2b, Sinderby. The presence of two chimney pots suggests that both the operating room and the locking room had fireplaces. It was unusual to heat the former. *Author's collection*

LEFT NSR Type 1, Sudbury. *Author*

ABOVE LMS Type 11c, Kettering Junction. Note the separate flight of stairs leading to the platform from which the tablet for the single line to and from Cambridge was handed out and collected. *Author*

RIGHT LNER Type non-standard, Connington North. *Kidderminster Railway Museum*

73

LEFT BR(ER) Type non-standard, Netherfield Junction. *Author*

RIGHT BR(SR) Type 16 at Shalford, next to an SER structure. *BR(SR)*

RIGHT BOTTOM BR(WR) Type 17 at Evesham Road Crossing, next to a GWR Type 4b at Stratford-upon-Avon Evesham Road Crossing. *Lens of Sutton collection*

BELOW BR(LMR) Type 15 at Dock Junction, next to an MR Type 2a. The brickwork of the new structure was laid to English bond standards. *BR(LMR)*

74

75

SHALFORD
SHALFORD

76

STRATFORD-UPON-AVON
EVESHAM ROAD CROSSING
EVESHAM ROAD CROSSING

77

LEFT The SDJR Type 2 signalboxes of the 1880s, of which that at West Pennard was an example, broke the accepted architectural conventions of the period by having windows with panes wider than they were tall. This gave the design a strangely mid-20th-century look. The style of barge-board shown here was also a distinctive feature of Somerset & Dorset signalboxes of the period. *J. Moss*

Attention to detail

The success of any model, be it of a locomotive or a building, is due not so much to absolute accuracy of scale as the effective representation of proportions. If all measurements on a model are correct in relation to each other, exact scale is of secondary importance. If one measurement is incorrect in comparison with others, the proportions are wrong and the model will not resemble the real thing; it will look odd. If all the passengers waiting on an 'OO'-gauge platform are actually 'HO' models, the discrepancy will probably not be noticed. However, if there is a mixture of 'OO' and 'HO' figures, the differences in proportion will be very obvious.

If you are attempting to model a particular style or known type of signalbox, the slavish replication of the prototype is not necessary to achieve authenticity, provided your model has the correct overall proportions and enough authentic features to convey the 'feel' of the real thing. Of course, your scope for latitude in interpretation diminishes when you model a signalbox produced by a railway company (notably the MR) that achieved standardisation in the majority of its structures. Get any element of a MR signalbox wrong and it will be as obvious as a standing model figure with arms that touch the ground, be it 'OO' or 'HO'. For example, with only three exceptions (on the Bradford–Shipley line), although the number of panes of glass in hundreds of MR signalbox window casements varied over the years each casement on the front of the structure always had a central, vertical glazing bar, the two 'compartments' so created having chamfered top corners. Get these features wrong and you cannot say your model is an MR structure. (There are a number of MR signalboxes illustrated in this book to support this observation.) By comparison, it is less demanding to model signalboxes in former LSWR territory because there were variations even within so-called 'standard' types. An authentic LSWR 'feel' can be achieved by incorporating only a few standard elements into a model, as long as the proportions are correct. Modellers are recommended to consult a copy of G. A. Pryer's *Signal Boxes of the London & South Western Railway* (Oakwood Press, 2000).

In the end, of course, it is for the modeller to decide to what lengths he/she is prepared to go to emulate the real thing. There is no law compelling you on pain of death to get the proportions of a standard MR signalbox right. If you model simply for pleasure and to please no one but yourself, and the critical comments of others do not matter, the goal of absolute accuracy becomes irrelevant. For those who are more demanding, the aim of the following is to draw your attention to those features that can give any model signalbox a truly authentic 'feel'.

Windows

In most traditional mechanical signalboxes the windows on the front and sides of the operating room (and sometimes the back) took the form of glazed timber casements. Each casement was usually glazed with a number of panes of glass separated and supported by wooden glazing bars. Usually the height of each pane was greater than its width – until the influence of 'modern' architecture took hold in the 1930s, when this long-held convention was reversed **[77]**. Getting the proportions of window panes correct will have a huge effect on the authentic look of a model signalbox.

Some signalboxes, notably those built during specific periods by the SER and NBR, were fitted with domestic sash windows, i.e. each window was formed of two casements arranged in a box frame so that the casements slid vertically over each other **[78**; *see* also **75]**. Without exception, when viewed from the outside of the structure the bottom casement was at the back of the box frame so that the top casement could slide in front of it. It was more common, however, to have casements fitted into box frames so that the casements slid horizontally. In a few signalboxes, notably NER Type S1 **[79]**, box frames containing just a pair of horizontally sliding casements were set individually into the walls. In most other signalbox designs the box frame was extended (along the entire length of the front of the structure) so that it could accommodate a row of casements. Sometimes all the casements could be slid open, whilst in other designs opening casements were interspersed with fixed units.

The reader might feel all this is either too obvious to be worth mentioning or is unnecessary information, but the main reason for labouring the point is that glazing bars and the arrangement of casements sliding across each other, either vertically or horizontally, has the effect of breaking up and giving depth to the overall glazing **[80]**. Traditional glazing made up of individual panes of glass and combinations of casements was never flat and was rarely flush with the supporting wall. The distribution of panes of glass in casements, the way casements are aligned, the distribution of fixed to opening units and the way in which they slide across each other are key features in differentiating one railway company style and type of

78

RIGHT Comparing this photograph of the NBR signalbox at Jedburgh with that of the signal hut at Belses [2] reveals that the use of standard domestic-type sash windows in the company's first fully interlocked signalboxes was a feature inherited from earlier structures. *R. K. Blencowe*

BELOW This photograph of Dawlish signalbox shows clearly that glazing in traditional, mechanical signalboxes was never 'flat' when there was the combination of sliding and fixed casements, all with timber glazing bars. *Author*

79

ABOVE The NER signalbox at Oxmardyke illustrates the standard arrangement of end windows, each with one fixed and one horizontally sliding casement, in structures of this type (S1a) built from the 1870s until 1903. *Author*

80

signalbox from another. Replicating windows effectively differentiates the very best models from the rest.

In the real world, over the past three decades these features have been disappearing rapidly as increasing numbers of old buildings, including signalboxes, have had their wooden framed windows replaced. Most replacements, of course, are made of PVC, but it has not been the use of this material that has destroyed the proportions of old buildings; it has been the loss of the changes of depth within a window. Nowadays casements are often set flush with the surrounding walls and the elimination of glazing bars or the attaching of mock bars on the inside (so as to leave the exterior smooth and thus cut down the time taken with cleaning) has the effect of emphasising the flatness of external glazing.

81

LEFT Hartlebury Station signalbox was for many years the last surviving example of a McKenzie & Holland Type 2 – until PVC replacement windows were fitted a few years ago. *Author*

BELOW Compared with Sutton Bridge Junction, the windows on the staircase end of Newton Abbot West signalbox illustrate the visually unsatisfactory results of slavish adherence by the GWR, between the wars, to the 'three-over-two' arrangement of glass panes. *Author*

82

RIGHT This photograph of the GWR signalbox at Sutton Bridge Junction, Shrewsbury, illustrates the best proportions of the company's characteristic 'three-over-two' glazing in individual casements. Also of interest are the differing degrees of weathering on the brickwork. *Author*

83

Another traditional glazing detail that has been altered where PVC windows are fitted, with both opening and fixed casements, is the size of the individual panes. With very few exceptions, when timber casements were arranged in a row, whether fixed or sliding, window panes were of the same size with the top and bottom of them in alignment horizontally. In modern PVC windows the opening casements usually have smaller panes, with the tops and bottoms out of alignment horizontally with their fixed neighbours [**81**].

To the relief of those readers who were about to abandon any attempt at signalbox modelling and write to the modelling press

84

to denounce the author as having a glazing fixation, the final example of authentic window design will come to their rescue. It concerns how in the real world one pre-1948 railway company – the GWR – manipulated the proportions of its last standard signalbox-window design (despite creating some badly proportioned casements as a result) purely in order to maintain a corporate 'house style'. The classic GWR pattern of 'three over two' panes in each casement first appeared in a signalbox in 1896. The initial intention was obviously to create almost square casements with one horizontal glazing bar just above the centre line, the bottom half of the casement being divided into two equal panes (with one vertical glazing bar) and the upper half split into three equal-sized panes (with two vertical glazing bars). The result was handsome [**82**]. So fond of this pattern of panes did the GWR become, however, that no alteration to the arrangement was made even if the casement was not square. Often on the end elevations of signalboxes, although casements were of the same height as on the front, they were narrower. In such cases it would have been sensible to fit only the horizontal glazing bar or one horizontal bar with the upper section divided with a single vertical bar, but the GWR stuck religiously to the 'three over two' arrangement, which often necessitated the fitting of very tall and narrow panes of glass. In the windows nearest the external door it was not uncommon to have casements fitted with the three top panes proportionally four times as high as they were wide [**83**]. Having made so much of how incorrect proportions can make something look 'odd', the author is bound to say that this certainly applied here. For modellers of the GWR, however, this is liberating information, because, no matter what height and width of casement they portray, as long as the 'three over two' panes arrangement is adopted, they will have authenticity on their side.

ABOVE Whoever designed the FR's signalboxes in the 1880s, of which St Bees is an example, obviously had an architect's eye. The tapered locking room of ashlar stonework and the pitch of the roof reveal that these structures were intended as more than merely functional buildings. This photograph dates from 1996; notice how the modern Portaloo has been disguised as a feature of the station garden. *Author*

85

RIGHT Even if not aspiring to grand architecture, almost every building of the mid- to late-Victorian era was well proportioned. The generous dimensions of the overhang of the roof of the GER signalbox at Attleborough provide just one example of how this was achieved. *Author*

ABOVE In a typical Victorian middle-class parlour the table would be draped with a heavy, tasselled cloth, as would the mantelpiece and any other piece of furniture with a flat top. The author cannot help feeling that the decorative awning on the LSWR's Feltham West signalbox is the equivalent of such a cloth, draped over the structure before the roof was fitted. *Lens of Sutton collection*

LEFT Like the GNR, the GER was fond of decorative barge-boards, but it used its own selection, this example, on March East signalbox of 1885, being used on other structures of this type built for the company by Saxby & Farmer in the 1880s. *Author*

Roofs

Another feature that must be modelled carefully if it is not to destroy the correct proportions of a building is the pitch of the roof. On the earliest signalboxes of the 1860s and early 1870s roofs with shallow pitches were almost universal, whether of the hipped or gabled variety. This feature was born of the fact signalboxes of this period were seen as basic utilitarian structures, no more than overgrown huts that did not fall within the definition of architecture. However, during the 1870s, as they evolved from being merely the products of joiners and carpenters to brick or stone structures erected by builders influenced by current architectural styles, their proportions began to alter, one of the most noticeable being the pitch of the roof [**84**].

The popularity of Gothic Revival architecture in the mid/late-Victorian period had an effect on even the most ordinary building with no obvious aspirations to grand architecture. On most classically inspired buildings roofs were either hidden behind parapets or kept shallow. However, on Gothic Revival buildings they were built to be admired, being generously proportioned and often with very steep pitches – features that found their way into many ordinary buildings, including signalboxes [**85**].

The Gothic Revival also influenced other features of many Victorian signalboxes in a more obvious way. Where simple gabled roofs were fitted, the ends were often adorned with decorative barge-boards. Many of these designs were based on boards fitted to domestic properties built in what has been termed the 'Cottage Orné' style. Most pre-Grouping railways had examples of signalboxes with decorative barge-boards, but they were particularly favoured by the GNR [*see* **37**, **93**], GER [**86**] and TVR. The design used on signalboxes supplied by the Railway Signal Co after its formation in 1881 became the equivalent of a trademark [*see* **51**].

ABOVE There was just enough room to fit decorative ridge tiles either side of a vent on the roof of the LNWR's 1875 Narborough signalbox. Author

89

LEFT It was good to see that in 2010 the ravages of the British weather and the results of recent 'risk assessments' had failed to dislodge the impressive finials of the LNWR's Beeston Castle & Tarporley signalbox, even though that immediately above the door to the operating room looks particularly menacing. *Author*

BELOW An enlargement from an Edwardian postcard, showing the fine detail of the finial and the well-made decorative barge-board on the lamp room adjacent to the GNR's The Hall signalbox, just west of Nottingham. Notice how the base of the GNR's finial is shaped like an acorn, contrasting with LNWR's 'arrow' at Beeston. Was this a conscious nod by the GNR to 'Health & Safety' [*see also* **37** *and* **93**]? *Author's collection*

On hipped roofs barge-boards could not be fitted, so to satisfy the Victorians' need for unnecessary ornamentation some railway companies (notably the LSWR and LBSCR) had decorative awnings (sometimes referred to as 'valences') fitted to the eaves of a number of their structures [**87**]. Even on some types of its gabled signalboxes the GER could not resist adding shallow awnings to their eaves.

Decorative, clay ridge tiles were also fitted on a few signalboxes, probably depending on their location rather than as a standard feature of a particular design type. They tended to appear where a structure was meant to impress, for example at an important town station [**88**; see also **10**]. The GWR proclaimed the importance of Reading as the centre for the manufacture of all its signalling needs from the end of the 19th century by adorning the huge West signalbox with a decorative ridge. Just how common decorative ridges were on the roofs of Victorian signalboxes is not certain. Where those fitted to signalboxes survived into the 20th century, photographic evidence reveals that over the years individual tiles had become damaged and the decorative feature knocked off, or that they were replaced altogether with plain tiles. This could indicate that complete decorative ridges had been replaced before they were recorded photographically. An official CR drawing of Rutherglen Loan Junction signalbox – reproduced as Plate 289 in *The Signal Box* (Signalling Study Group/OPC, 1986) – indicates that a decorative iron grille was to be fitted on the ridge of this structure's roof, but that must have been a very unusual feature.

Finials were more popular both for finishing off the end ridges of gabled roofs and marking the point where the three sides of a hipped roof met. Even the dour LNWR, which generally eschewed

90

91

unnecessary decoration, succumbed to the fad for finials [**89**]. Most companies, if they had them at all, fitted fine timber examples [**90**], but terracotta finials were not uncommon [**91**]. In model form the proportions of finials can make or break the authentic look of a structure. Too tall, and they begin to look like lightning conductors; too small, and they look as though they might have been damaged in a session of sky shunting.

The lighting of signalboxes with oil lamps persuaded some companies and signalling contractors that roof vents were a necessity. The inevitable variety of styles clearly indicates the owning company or the firm that built the structure [see **2**, **42** and **63**].

Nameboards

Pre-Grouping railway companies displayed the names of their signalboxes in a variety of ways and with lettering of noticeably differing styles and sizes. All but the GNR attached the name to the front of a signalbox, usually on the lower storey. Sensibly, but with an uncharacteristic disregard for economy, the GNR fitted a board to each end of its signalboxes so that approaching train crews could see them.

Victorian and Edwardian photographs show that two of the earliest preferences for marking signalboxes were with sign-written boards [**92**] or enamelled plates, the latter used by the NER, GER, SER, MR, GNR [**93**] and MGNJR. By the beginning of the 20th century, however, by far the most popular method of identification was the use of cast-iron letters, either screwed directly onto the structure [**94**] or, more commonly, attached to wooden boards [**95**, **96**].

ABOVE The FR chose to use terracotta finials on a number of its signalboxes, as here at Arnside. *Author*

BELOW Many Victorian and Edwardian photographs are so clear that details, obviously incidental when the original image was taken, can now prove very useful for the modeller. Only an indication of colour is missing from this fine example of signwriting on the LBSCR's Selsdon Road North signalbox. The bricks are laid Flemish bond with (typically) very fine pointing. *Author's collection*

92

93

Needless to say, the GWR took the whole idea of cast-iron lettering a stage further than did other companies, its belief in standardisation and the virtues of 'built to last' leading to the production of hundreds of cast-iron boards **[97]**. Usually there was just one, on the front of a signalbox, but where running lines passed behind as well, another was provided on that elevation. When the LMS and subsequently the LMR and other regions of the new British Railways began to adopt the GNR practice of attaching boards at either end of signalboxes the GWR standard remained unchanged, much as the WR succeeded in retaining its cast locomotive numberplates.

Between the wars the SR also continued to attach names to the front of signalboxes but obviously believed that increasing their size would provide better visibility for staff and passengers on passing trains. On new 'Glasshouse' signalboxes the lettering was cast in concrete, but elsewhere enamel boards were used to match the company's up-to-date branding of other buildings.

Following the formation of British Railways in 1948, enamel boards found their way first onto new signalboxes built by the Eastern Region **[98]** and then more widely across the country on both new structures and as replacement to older boards **[99]**. At first their colour scheme adhered to the corporate identity of the particular region, but by the beginning of the 1970s simpler white boards with black lettering became the standard throughout the country – the first time signalbox names had not been rendered entirely in upper-case lettering.

ABOVE In tender documents of the 1870s the GNR specified that blue-and-white enamel nameplates should be fitted to its signalboxes. The pair at Honington Junction survived until the signalbox was closed in 1984. Take note of that full stop! *Author*

94

RIGHT The beautifully preserved Frome Mineral Junction at Didcot Railway Centre shows how GWR signalboxes were marked before cast-iron plates became standard. Also of note is the well-executed Flemish bond brickwork with, unfortunately, 'generous' post-World War 2 pointing. *Author*

95

96

ABOVE Reepham signalbox, photographed a few years before the 1923 Grouping, displaying its standard MSLR nameboard. As with the GNR's board at Honington Junction, a full stop is included. *Author's collection*

LEFT After 1923 the LNER felt it necessary to rename Reepham signalbox so that staff and locals would not erroneously think it was controlling trains in both Lincolnshire and at Reepham, Norfolk. Although 'Lincs' is obviously an abbreviation, no full stop was wasted on this new board (or that on the opposite side of the signalbox). *Author*

BELOW An example of the GWR's standard cast-iron signalbox nameboard at Gobowen North, still in situ in 1996. *Author*

97

98

99

ABOVE The new (1957) signalbox at Sleaford South was fitted with three enamel nameboards, the staircase elevation being the only one to remain anonymous. *BR(ER)*

BELOW Many of the signalboxes inherited by BR's London Midland Region were fitted with new enamel nameboards in corporate regional colours, the ex-MR signalbox at Skipton North being a typical example. *Author*

4 Inside the signalbox

The inside of the signalbox might be considered one of the most difficult areas for the modeller. Firstly there is the question of whether or not to fit an interior at all and then, if internal fittings are considered necessary, of what they should be.

As with all aspects of modelling, the larger the gauge, the more obvious the omissions. In 'N' gauge only a few people will feel compelled to fit out their signalboxes, but as soon as the scale increases, a building with large expanses of glazing, allowing the spectator a good view inside, becomes conspicuous if it is empty. Unless you are modelling Southern Region art-deco structures the majority of station buildings have small windows, conveniently removing the need to fit interiors. In model towns only the shop windows need be filled, and large church windows can legitimately be obscured with stained and painted glass to prevent any glimpse of the interior. But most traditional signalboxes were built as observation towers with plenty of glass to give signalmen a clear view of the area under their control. In any gauge above 'N', not fitting out your signalbox could be seen as the equivalent of not providing the footplates of your steam locomotives with controls, now a standard feature on every new ready-to-run model.

Some modellers might feel that there is an excessive amount of detailed and unnecessary information in this chapter, given how little might be visible, irrespective of gauge, in a model structure that will usually be viewed from above. The author's justification is that as a number of manufacturers already supply components for model-signalbox interiors in a variety of gauges, and, as quite a number of modellers are very proud to lift the roof from their signalbox to show off the interior, people deserve to know if what they see is realistic.

Given the complexity of the subject, it is quite understandable that many modellers struggle to achieve authenticity. This is not just because what is provided in interior-detailing kits can never exactly match the track layout of every model; the problem arises with the combination of levers and electrical instrumentation. All too often, when the roof is raised what is revealed is the equivalent of a steam-locomotive footplate with four regulator handles, two firebox holes, six boiler-pressure gauges and a clock. Therefore, in the spirit of constructive criticism rather than condemnation, this chapter aims, among other things, to explain the basic mechanical and electrical

BELOW An early 20th century photograph of the interior of a large LNWR signalbox. Although it provides an impressive view that might be expected to help the modeller, it is in reality of limited use save to establish 'atmosphere'. *Author's collection*

100

components and what they do and to examine how they all fit together. Hopefully the modeller prepared to undertake a bit of 'cutting and pasting' of proprietary products and a little inventive scratch-building will then end up with something that looks authentic.

Ironically, one of the problems for the modeller arises from the wealth of interior photographs of signalboxes. Why? Because given the inherent difficulties of taking photographs inside buildings, the majority were taken in large signalboxes with lots of levers and a mass of instrumentation that even to some signalling experts can defy explanation [**100**]. When it comes to the small, typical mechanical signalboxes with a few levers and even fewer electrical instruments that would act as more typical prototypes for most models, photographs tend to be of the signalman posing proudly outside on the steps, or leaning out of the operating-room window. The interior is frustratingly hidden.

The lack of 'typical' evidence is compounded by the fact that most photographs that might be useful were taken in black and white. The modeller then knows what it must have been like in the 18th and 19th century to be interested in art but unable to travel and have to rely on monochrome prints of the great masters' works. Was that saint dressed in a red robe the colour of a home signal, or was it in fact a blue one, the hue of a facing-point locking lever?

Another deceptive thing with photographs of large mechanical signalboxes is the impression they give that railway companies were generous in their provision of equipment, just because there is obviously so much of it on show. The modeller needs to be cautious. Victorian companies were very, very careful with expenditure. Railways did not spend money on equipment if they felt it was unnecessary. What drove improvements to signalling was the desire to control traffic more efficiently, to increase line capacity whilst at the same time preventing accidents, which would involve government inspectors, lawyers and the settlement of potentially costly insurance claims.

Throughout the 19th century the Board of Trade exerted steady pressure to improve railway safety, and its influence tended to increase the level of equipment both inside signalboxes and at the lineside. But this was a protracted process, and the interiors of signalboxes of the 1870s were fitted with less mechanical and electrical equipment than they would be at the end of that century. The zenith of mechanical signalling was reached in the early years of the 20th century, the Locomotive Yard signalbox just south of York station, built by the NER in 1909 to house one continuous frame of 295 levers, being the longest ever built. After that the odd extra lever might be added to a frame, or a replacement might be slightly larger, requiring the extension of a signalbox, but any noticeable increase in signalbox equipment was on the electrical side. But even here the modeller needs to be careful. Between the two world wars many signalboxes retained either the original or exactly the same type of block instruments with which they had been fitted in the 1870s and '80s. In fact until the 1960s, there were almost certainly more block instruments of 19th century design in use than those of post-1900 configuration. The most visible sign of change in the years leading up to nationalisation was in the increasing use of signal repeaters and track-circuit indicators (*see below*). This trend continued after 1948, until illuminated diagrams (*see below*) became more common, eliminating the need for individual track-circuit indicators.

Part 1 Mechanical equipment

Every signalbox erected from the early 1870s to the end of the Victorian era – and the majority of those constructed between then and the 1960s – would have been equipped with mechanical levers to work signals, points and other miscellaneous mechanical devices.

Levers

Levers were arranged in frames so that they could be mechanically linked – 'interlocked' – to prevent the random movement of levers that might give conflicting indications to drivers and cause accidents.

As a general rule (and certainly as far as modellers need concern themselves) each lever worked one piece of equipment, and the number of levers in a model signalbox will reflect the complexity of the track layout it is purporting to control. The number of signals at the lineside and the number of points/turnouts connected with the main running lines will equate roughly to the number of levers in the 'box. There are, naturally, exceptions, perhaps the most relevant (and commonplace) being that, in most signalboxes, crossovers, although physically two points/turnouts, were operated by just one lever.

The normal position of levers would have been nearly upright, a lever being pulled forward (reversed) by the signalman to change the indication of a signal from 'danger' to 'all clear' or the position of a point/turnout. Here is the first challenge for the modeller – getting the correct inclination of a lever when it is reversed. In all but a handful of designs the fulcrum (pivot) of the lever was a few feet below the floor of the operating room in which the signalman worked. What you see in the operating room is in reality only part of the full length of a lever emerging through cast metal 'quadrant plates' from the locking room below. Therefore, when setting your model lever you have to imagine that 'extra' length and the arc that would be described from a fulcrum set beneath the place where the signalman stands [**101**].

From the 1870s it was generally the case that only points/turnouts and signals on through running lines were controlled from signalboxes. Once trains had been turned off main lines into sidings or yards they became the responsibility of their crews and shunters, points/turnouts being operated by hand levers on the ground. Before the end of the 19th century it was also true that not every movement on the main through lines immediately adjacent to signalboxes was controlled by a mechanical signal operated by a lever in the box, flags and lamps often being used by signalmen to authorise trains through crossovers before shunting signals ('dollies' etc) were provided. Just to reiterate, railway companies were careful not to spend money on what they believed was unnecessary equipment.

The tendency by the end of the 19th century was to provide more shunting signals controlled from signalboxes as well as 'calling-on' signals to regulate movements in busy stations. (Being such a prosperous company, the North Eastern Railway was particularly keen on these). As a consequence late-Victorian and early-Edwardian signalboxes, particularly at principal stations, were usually larger than their predecessors because more levers had to be accommodated inside.

The trend towards ever-larger installations led some progressive signal engineers to experiment with alternative methods of operating points and signals from other than mechanical levers. In use by the beginning of the 20th century were a number of pneumatic,

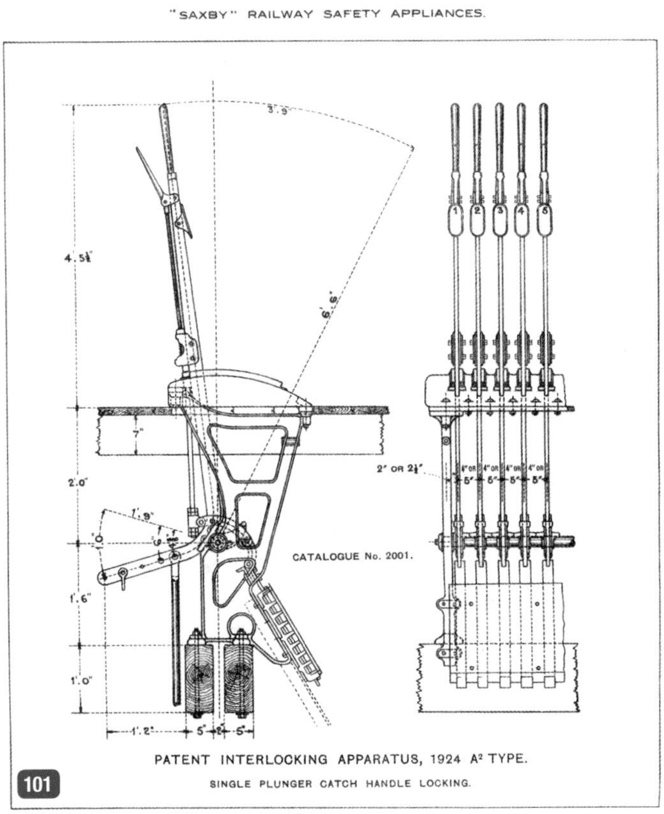

"SAXBY" RAILWAY SAFETY APPLIANCES.
CATALOGUE No. 2001.
PATENT INTERLOCKING APPARATUS, 1924 A² TYPE.
SINGLE PLUNGER CATCH HANDLE LOCKING.

101

ABOVE A page from a 1929 Westinghouse Brake & Saxby Signal Co catalogue, showing two sections through the company's standard A2 lever frame [*see* **104**]. *Author's collection*

102

RIGHT The LNWR's design of miniature lever frame, with two rows of levers, meant it occupied far less space than an equivalent 'full-size' frame with the same number of levers. This photograph was taken inside Crewe North signalbox in the 1930s. *LMS*

electro-pneumatic and electrical systems in which levers had been miniaturised [**102**] or replaced by mechanical 'slides' working in the horizontal plane with grasp handles [**103**]. Both miniature levers and slides could be grouped closer together than conventional levers, thus reducing the length of signalboxes.

But before we get carried away with history and specialist developments let us return to the ubiquitous lever frame. From a modelling perspective, the earlier the period you have chosen to represent, the fewer the levers that will be needed and, consequently, the smaller the signalbox itself. The more complex the track layout, for example at termini, the more levers and the bigger the structure required.

The next aspect that will affect the authentic appearance of the levers inside your model signalbox is their spacing in the frame. Although in modelling terms we are talking about only a few millimetres between accuracy and inaccuracy, for some people this can be as important as the difference between 'OO'- and 18.83-gauge track.

103

RIGHT The pneumatic frame, with its pull-out slides, installed in the GCR's Elsecar Junction signalbox in the first decade of the 20th century. *Dr J. W. F. Scrimgeour/ Kidderminster Railway Museum (SE153/6)*

LEFT The Westinghouse lever frame inside the SR signalbox at Minster, photographed shortly after the 'box opened in 1929. Notice the huge illuminated diagram, the hand-painted lever-description plates, lettered in black or white, and the fact there are repeaters above most of the levers operating signals (the cylindrical shapes fitted to the front of the block shelf). *Author's collection*

ABOVE An example of a Ransome & Rapier 'hayrake' lever frame, inside the GNR signalbox at Hubberts Bridge. *Dr J. W. F. Scrimgeour/Kidderminster Railway Museum (SE208/2)*

The spaces between each lever – the pitch (usually expressed as the measurement from the centres of adjacent levers) – varied depending on which railway company or signalling contractor manufactured the equipment. The largest space was 6in (152mm), a standard rigidly adhered to by the MR, for example, but also used in frames made by other signalling contractors and railway companies from the early 1870s until the 1890s. The smallest gap was just 3½in (89mm), chosen by the ever-cost-conscious Great Northern Railway for a handful of frames it manufactured itself. A common pitch was 4in (102mm), a feature of all frames made by the GWR at its Reading works between 1908 and the 1960s, for example, and of the Railway Signal Co's and Saxby & Farmer's last frame designs, the latter perpetuated under Westinghouse management and used extensively by the LNER and SR [**104**; *see also* **101**]. If we compare a standard MR frame of 16 levers with an equivalent run of 16 levers in a late-GWR design of frame (including 6in and 4in respectively at either end) the length of the former is 8ft 6in (2.6m), the equivalent of 34mm in 4mm gauge, and the latter 5ft 8in (1.7m), the equivalent of 23.2mm. Those millimetres will make a visual difference!

As mentioned in a previous chapter, MR signalboxes were constructed of standard-size timber panels, which meant that the lever frames did not influence the length of signalboxes as directly as it did for those of companies like the GNR, which until the start of the 20th century tolerated much more variety in frame design, the number of levers and the dimensions of signalboxes being very often dependent upon local conditions (as well as the builder employed).

Another feature of frame design that can be very noticeable in model form if incorrectly reproduced also concerns the MR and the GNR, as well as signalling contractor Saxby & Farmer. In the majority of frames the interlocking was out of sight in the locking room and is therefore irrelevant from a modelling perspective. But there were four exceptions. The first was not at all common and was confined almost exclusively to the GNR, but if modelled well it would make a wonderful talking-point. In the 1870s, at a number of locations, the GNR installed a frame designed and manufactured by Ransome & Rapier, favoured because it was so much cheaper than any other then available. The frame sat on the operating-room floor, with every part of its mechanism exposed, and was nicknamed the 'hayrake' on account of its resemblance to that particular piece of agricultural equipment. The locking was in front of the levers in just the right position to trap a signalman's trousers or braces as he leaned over to reach for the catch handle [**105**], but despite this and numerous other drawbacks the last example (at Rauceby in Lincolnshire) was not taken out of use until 1975.

The second exception was a configuration of interlocking used by the LNWR in its overhead signalboxes. The basic mechanism did not differ from that employed in standard signalboxes except that it was positioned vertically behind the levers, such that it resembled a screen made up of latter-day fencing panels.

The last two exceptions to the rule were less eccentric and more widespread. In Saxby & Farmer's 'Rocker & Gridiron' and MR frames the locking was immediately behind the levers. In the former it was exposed at operating floor level [**106**], but in MR frames, although it was again behind the levers, it was housed at about knee-level within the main body of the frame which also contained the lever pivots. This arrangement gave MR frames a very distinctive appearance [*see* **108**], almost like long, metal benches in a waiting room, and this is important for modellers, because if they fit the wrong frame into a standard MR signalbox the mistake is very obvious.

Until the 20th century, regardless of design, it was standard practice for lever frames to be positioned at the front of signalboxes, invariably parallel with the track. This meant that signalmen could operate levers whilst still keeping an eye on activities outside. But as more equipment (i.e. block instruments and signal repeaters) was fitted above frames and when layout diagrams increased in size to accommodate track-circuit lights (*see below*) the view became obscured, and consequently it was felt desirable to reposition

ABOVE A view showing the interlocking located immediately behind the levers of the Saxby & Farmer 'Rocker & Gridiron' lever frame inside the GNR's Bellwater Junction signalbox. *Author*

everything to the back of the 'box. This trend started just before World War 1, and by the 1930s most new signalboxes conformed to the new arrangement; a few older structures were similarly rearranged when frames needed replacement. So from a modelling point of view it would be legitimate to have a Victorian signalbox with a frame at the back of the structure on a layout of the 1950s. Even more exciting would be a 'box in transition, with a replacement frame fitted but the old one still in use.

With the lever frame in place we should now consider how the signalman knew which lever operated which piece of equipment. The relationship of colour to function was established early in the history of signalboxes, and from the 1870s there appears to have been a general agreement between railway companies and the Board of Trade as to what colour levers should be painted. By the Grouping of 1923 the following colours were used throughout the country, and most remain the standard wherever mechanical signalling is still in use.

BELOW Because the lever frame in Sleaford North signalbox controls a double-line junction there are three levers operating distant signals – No 1 the down branch distant, No 3 the down main distant, and No 18 the up distant. The last being a colour-light signal, the top of the lever has been cut down to indicate that it has no mechanical function and is acting purely as an electrical switch; as Nos 5 and 11 have been treated in the same way they too must be electrical switches. Blue lever No 6 is reversed because it is locking the junction's facing point, operated by lever No 7. *Author*

Stop signals, including shunting signals	*red*
Stop signal released by 'Line Clear'	*red with horizontal white stripe*
Distant signals	*green (pre-1925) yellow (post-1925)*
Intermediate Block signals	*red (top) yellow (bottom)*
Points	*black*
Facing-point locks	*blue*
Facing points with combined locks	*blue and black*
Gate locks	*brown*
Detonator placers	*black and white chevrons, pointing upwards for up lines and down for down lines*
Spare/non-operational	*white*

As with all aspects of railway operation, there were, of course, exceptions, but none sufficiently significant to merit mention here [**107**].

Modellers seeking to achieve absolute accuracy with their signalbox will concern themselves not merely with the number and colours of levers, reflecting the amount and function of lineside equipment; they will wish also to distribute the levers correctly within the frame. Taking a double section of main line as an example, if you are modelling a Victorian signalbox at any time in its history the distant signal levers will almost always be at opposite ends of the frame, with red levers operating home and starting signals next in line. Any levers operating points/turnouts and disc signals will be located towards the centre of the frame. The order in which the main running-line signals – i.e. distant, home, starting – are fitted into the frame will always reflect their geographical positions outside by the lineside. So, imagining you are a model signalman looking at his lever frame operating that combination of signals for each direction, at the left-hand end of the frame you have, from left to right, distant, home, starting and at the right-hand end of the frame, from left to right, starting, home, distant. There should be no other non-signal levers interrupting that sequence – only additional signal levers if required, e.g. outer distant, distant, outer home, home, starting, advance starting. (As might be expected, the precise nomenclature varied between railways.)

There are two common exceptions to the 'distant-signal levers at the end of the frame' rule. If your signalbox controls gates at a level crossing the distant-signal lever would not be at the very end of the frame nearer the crossing, that position being occupied by one or two levers to lock and unlock the gate stops and sometimes a couple more levers if there were additional wicket gates or if the main gates were operated by a wheel in the 'box [*see* **114**, **115**]. Sometimes there was a separate frame with a pair of levers for the wicket gates.

The second exception to the rule arises in the case of more modern signalboxes or where a lever frame had been relocked or, more likely, replaced (as might have happened at some time immediately before or at any time after World War 1). In such cases it would be legitimate to have the distant, home and starting signal levers for up and down lines nearer the centre, with shunting-signal and point levers either side [**108**]. However, the rule concerning the geographical position of the main running-line signals would still apply (i.e. distant-signal levers at the extremities of the group of levers).

Because post-1925 yellow distant-signal levers at either end of a model frame inside a signalbox can be quite noticeable, the one thing you must avoid if you aspire to authenticity is having the distant-signal lever reversed (pulled towards the signalman) when all the other, red levers next to it are in their normal position (i.e. not reversed), as in a real signalbox the interlocking would have prevented such a configuration; you can, however, legitimately have all the home and starting levers reversed while the distant-signal lever is in the normal position.

Finally, at termini it would be unusual to have working distant signals, so yellow levers are the last thing you want to see through the windows of your model signalbox at such locations.

We turn now to the subject of levers painted black, to indicate that they are operating points/turnouts. If you are claiming that some are working facing points there should always be a blue locking lever immediately next to each one, unless you are modelling a combined facing-point and lock lever, as favoured by the MR – in which case the top half of the lever should be blue, the bottom half black.

Mention of the colour for combined facing-point and lock levers leads to the last little subtlety that might or might not be worth the effort of modelling. The first 'dual action' levers encountered by this

ABOVE Garsdale signalbox, opened in 1910, had its lever frame fitted at the back of the 'box, the main running-line signals being grouped in the centre of the frame, as seen here. The block shelf has a standard array of block instruments for controlling a section of double track, including two MR rotary peggers that were finally replaced by standard BR modular instruments in September 2002. *Author*

author operated motor-worked facing points and had the tops of the handles cut down by a few inches to indicate that they were, in effect, electrical switches and did not need to be pulled or pushed as hard as levers working mechanical devices. Reducing the height of levers activating colour-light signals – or semaphores or points worked by motors – became a standard feature after World War 1 as more of this equipment was installed. Where electrically operated equipment and new frames were installed at the same time, manufacturers supplied levers with small tops that matched those of their full-height mechanical neighbours [*see* **104**]. This was so much more aesthetically pleasing than the results of the on-site hack-sawing of older frames – something the author remembers on the former GNR main line in the 1970s. So, if you are really keen to show off your signalling knowledge and have a few colour-light signals on your layout, hack the tops off a few levers in the signalbox. And if you model the GN main line in the 1970s, make sure that none of the tops of the cut-down levers are the same height!

Obviously, colour alone was not enough to indicate which lever operated which specific piece of equipment in a signalbox. Common to every lever frame was the numbering of levers consecutively from left to right, starting with '1'. The only exceptions were where extra

ABOVE A clear view of some of the lever plates on the Railway Signal Co frame fitted inside the GCR signalbox at Marylebone station. The cast-iron plates have the lever's number at the top, the numbers of other levers in the 'pulling sequence' being listed beneath, while the function of each lever is neatly hand-lettered on the timber board running the length of the frame immediately behind the levers. The vertical rod with the 'crank handle' top (right) is for altering the tension of a signal wire. *Author's collection*

ABOVE Interior of the preserved LBSCR signalbox at Horsted Keynes as it appeared in the early 1980s, with hand-painted lever-number/description plates attached low down, close to the quadrant plate. The black wheel attached to the end wall is for adjusting the tension of the wire to the down advance home signal, operated by lever No 13. *Author*

levers had been added at the left-hand end of the frame; usually the railway company labelled these using letters, but very occasionally, if only one extra lever had been added (and the author can think of only the GWR as an example), the lever could be labelled '0'.

What varied considerably between the frames of pre-Grouping companies was whether or not the lever number was physically separate from the description of its function. Where the number was not part of the description it was engraved on a brass plate or cast into a brass or cast-iron plate, usually attached on the front of the lever close to the pivot of the catch handle. Needless to say, these plates varied in outline from circular to lollipop-shaped. The latter had evolved out of the need to list the numbers of other levers that had to be operated by the signalman before he could pull that particular lever, this list being on the 'stick' part of the lollipop [**109**].

Some companies attached larger plates – either brass or cast-iron – which bore the lever number at the top, followed by a description of what that lever operated and then usually the numbers of the other levers in the 'pulling sequence'. All this information was painted on, engraved or sometimes cast into the plates. After the Grouping it was standard practice on the SR and LNER to use such hand-painted plates, the SR preferring to position them at the base of the lever [**110**], the LNER almost always affixing them just beneath the catch-handle pivot. Both companies' plates were of broadly the same shape and size, the majority 3in (75mm) wide by 8in (203mm) deep, all with semi-circular tops and either flat or semi-circular bottoms. The plates were painted the same colour as the lever, with numbers and lettering in either black or white.

This form of combined lever-number and description plate had been inherited by the SR from the LBSCR, and by the LNER from GNR and GER practice. On Southern lines, well into BR days,

111

ABOVE Part of the lever frame inside the preserved GWR signalbox at Bewdley South, photographed in the early 1980s. Typical engraved brass lever plates of various lengths can be seen alongside later standard-length 'Traffolite' examples. On the block shelf are two standard GWR Absolute Block instruments of 1947 design and two 'banner' track-circuit repeaters. *Author*

112

ABOVE This photograph of the interior of the MR's Dock Junction signalbox was taken in 1956, shortly before the 'box closed, and shows how in the earliest MR frames, dating from the 1870s, a lever's function was engraved on a brass plate attached to its right-hand side. *BR(LMR)*

the plates continued to be hand-painted (the quality of calligraphy having declined noticeably by the 1960s), but by the 1930s the LNER was using machine-engraved 'Traffolite' plates that were screwed onto either the existing plates or new cast-iron supports. Under BR management 'Traffolite' plates were used also in a few SR signalboxes when descriptions needed to be altered. Both types of combined plate were large compared with those of other companies, so their absence in model form will be quite obvious.

The GWR also standardised on a combined number and description plate, but until the 1940s these were of engraved brass. Unlike the plates used by the LNER and SR they varied quite noticeably in length depending on the number of other levers in a 'pulling sequence' that had to be recorded [**111**]. In large signalboxes some plates were almost as long as the levers to which they were attached. During and after World War 2 the ubiquitous 'Traffolite' plate began to make its appearance in GWR signalboxes. This was made slightly wider than its brass predecessor (though not as wide as those used by the LNER) in a largely successful attempt to ensure standardisation of length.

In contrast the LMS, by allowing the standards of its pre-Grouping companies to continue (with a little modernisation creeping in by the end of the 1930s), had completely different standards. In the majority of LMS signalboxes the lever number was separate from the description of function. When Saxby & Farmer had started to supply the LNWR with lever frames in the 1860s each had come with one brass plate the length of the frame, carefully engraved with all the lever functions and attached at floor level behind the levers and angled towards the signalman. The disadvantage, of course, was that if lever functions changed either a new plate had to be engraved or, more usually, the original had to be patched in some way.

Similar long horizontal plates were supplied with other signalling contractors' frames, notably those made by McKenzie & Holland and the Railway Signal Co, but these were wooden, with hand-painted descriptions, which could be modified more easily if lever functions changed. When the LNWR started to manufacture its own frames from the middle of the 1870s, instead of hand-lettering the boards behind the levers it cast small rectangular plates with the appropriate descriptions for each lever and screwed these to the board. The plates were painted in the same colour as the levers they described. The same practice was adopted by the LYR when it started to make its own frames in the 1890s, many of its earliest frames having also been supplied by Saxby & Farmer with brass plates and then, during the 1880s, by the Railway Signal Co with hand-painted description boards.

On the first MR frames of the 1870s tiny brass plates only the width of the part of the lever facing the signalman were engraved with the number. In model form these would be almost impossible to see in any gauge below 'O'. Larger plates eventually appeared, 30mm in width. Initially descriptions were engraved on long brass plates attached to the right-hand side of the levers, and although this practice was long-lived [**112**] the method most commonly adopted by the time of the Grouping was to fix rectangular brass plates (130mm high by 100mm wide) to the covers over the interlocking behind the levers. In LMS days there appeared aluminium or white-metal equivalents, and under BR management any new plates were of the 'Traffolite' variety.

113

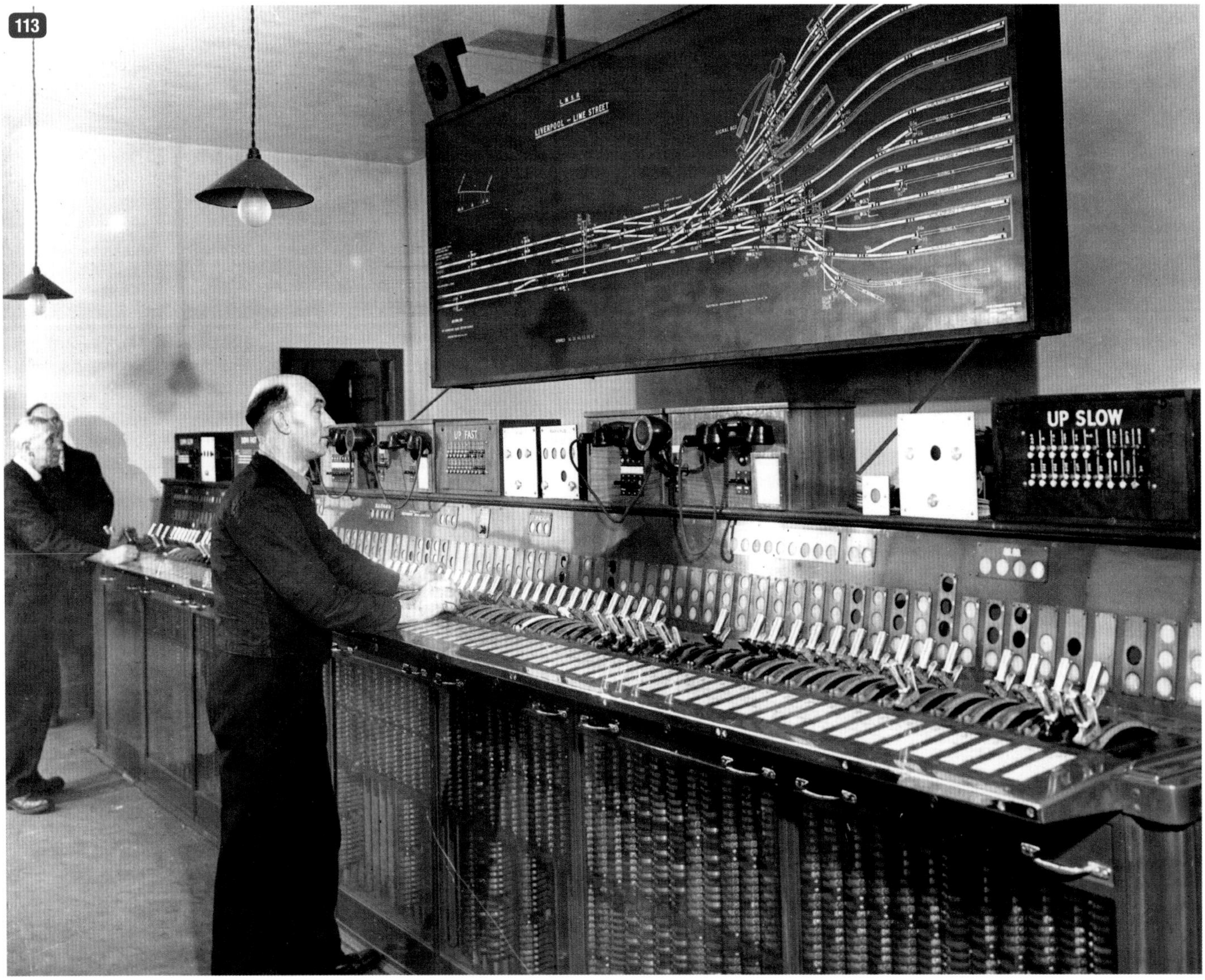

ABOVE The miniature lever frame inside the new Liverpool Lime Street signalbox of 1948. The circular lights behind each lever indicated whether or not the piece of equipment had responded correctly to the operation of that lever. *BR(LMR)*

Power frames

At the very end of the 19th century new types of equipment appeared for operating signals and points/turnouts. Their design and appearance was very distinctive, and as these special pieces of equipment were used in so few locations compared with traditional lever frames you will need a very good reason to model them [*see* **102**, **132**]; you will be representing either a real location or somewhere on the fringes of where you might be able to justify the installation of similar equipment. And if you are going to all that trouble, remember there will have to be appropriate lineside equipment with air cylinders or electric motors to work signals and points/turnouts.

After World War 1 and until the end of the 1930s these 'power frames' were not considered as unusual as they had once been. There were two basic designs (which varied, of course) – one with horizontal pull-out slides, each with a grasp-handle [*see* **103**], the other with miniature levers [**113**]. Either slides or levers were set at between stomach and chest height into a rectangular cabinet or open frame containing all the appropriate switches, cables, pipes, relays, valves, etc. Slides protruded from the front, whilst miniature levers were arranged along the top of the cabinet or frame. Like full-size levers, what little shank the slides or miniature levers had was painted the appropriate colour for its function (see above).

In early installations block instruments, along with other relevant electrical equipment, were positioned over these frames on traditional shelves. During the 1930s, however, the GWR designed a set of art-deco-style instrumentation that was integrated into the main cabinet, and this marked the beginning of the development of the modern signalling 'panel', which will be examined later.

Miscellaneous mechanical equipment

Levers used to place detonators on the line in an emergency were not always fitted into the main lever frame. The GWR, for example, often provided a separate two-lever frame for working detonator placers. A noticeable feature of many lever frames used by the LNER were stirrups for operating detonator placers fitted just above the quadrant plates – a useful trip hazard for those signalmen in the habit of walking along the quadrant plates to answer block bells.

ABOVE If a wheel were specified for operating the crossing gates at a signalbox, McKenzie & Holland could supply a lever frame with that wheel attached at one end. This example was still operational in the ex-NER signalbox at Filey when photographed in 1988. *Author*

ABOVE Seen here inside the GNR's Grand Sluice signalbox at Boston is an example of that railway's preferred design of wheel for operating crossing gates, even though the McKenzie & Holland lever frame has the appropriate quadrant plate for fixing that company's standard mechanism. *Author*

Probably the most distinctive piece of miscellaneous equipment in certain signalboxes was the 'gate wheel'. Used to open and shut level crossing gates from the signalbox, needless to say they came in various shapes and sizes. Some, as used by the LNWR, MR, MSLR and NER for example, resembled ships' wheels [**114**]. Others, such as those preferred by the GNR, were more akin to cast-iron mangles used for wringing water out of clothes [**115**].

Mechanisms for altering the tension of signal wires were positioned either behind the lever frame, through the quadrant plates or more conveniently at the ends of the frame. As you would expect, every railway company before the 1923 Grouping had its preferred design of equipment [*see* **109**]. Some used a vertical rod with ratchet, grasped using a stirrup handle and either pulled up to apply tension or, by releasing the ratchet, let drop to slacken the wire. Another design comprised a vertical pillar containing a treaded bar worked by a horizontal wheel on the top. Both these varieties were free-standing, but another common arrangement was the vertical cast-iron wheel (with ratchet) that was attached either to the wall or woodwork beneath the windows of the signalbox [*see* **110**]. The wheels were either turned directly by hand or via a worm gear arrangement turned by the insertion of a 'T'-handled rod. If signalboxes had two working distant signals it usually followed that they also had at least two wire-adjusters. For the modeller the general rule should be to include such equipment only if there are signals at some considerable distance from the signalbox or around sharp curves.

Also prominent inside some signalboxes were mechanical signal and/or slot indicators. Connected to signals worked from adjacent signalboxes, slot indicators showed whether or not those signals had been operated. Such information could govern how or when signals in the signalbox receiving it were worked, depending upon the regulations in force at that particular location. Some pre-Grouping railway companies installed slot indicators mounted on pillars, whilst others, such as the MR, attached them a few inches above the operating floor [*see* **124**]. By the end of the 1930s, unless signalboxes were already fitted with the equipment, mechanical indicators had been superseded by electrical indicators.

Part 2 Electrical equipment

The mysteries of electrical equipment in signalboxes, particularly what should appear on block shelves, have defeated many a modeller (and manufacturer) – more so than has been the case with mechanical equipment. Despite numerous books on signalling, model block shelves still sport all sorts of miscellaneous rectangular boxes, so, as regurgitating real-life procedures will probably not improve this, a different approach is adopted here.

Let us start by recalling that until the 20th century, signalboxes contained very little electrical equipment – just block instruments and block bells to regulate the passage of trains and perhaps one or two telegraph instruments for sending and receiving other messages. Until the 20th century, other than at busier locations, it was not usual to have any other specialist electrical instruments, although they were available. Single-line instruments, signal repeaters, lamp indicators, point indicators, train describers, track-circuit indicators, illuminated diagrams and telephones were all there to be used by signal engineers by the 1890s, but railway managers were worried about initial cost, then the use of continuous battery power and all the additional maintenance, not to mention the belief held by some that signalmen would rely too heavily on equipment and become less vigilant. The concern was that devices would give staff the opportunity to absolve themselves of blame if something went wrong, citing 'instrument failure'.

Absolute Block instruments and block bells

Block instruments and block bells were used to control the passage of trains between signalboxes. The instruments would have been found in every signalbox controlling trains on single lines between the 1860s and about the first decade of the 20th century, depending on the railway company, and all signalboxes post-1860 controlling multiple lines worked by Absolute or Permissive Block regulations.

When, in the late 1860s, block instruments and block bells were first brought together with lever frames in signalboxes they were usually located separately, the instruments often on cupboards (containing the batteries) or on shelves opposite the lever frame [**116**]. It was not until the 1880s that shelves for instruments were positioned over lever frames. The shelf was either suspended on rods from the roof trusses, sometimes supplemented by supports from the floor or the lever frame itself (some of McKenzie & Holland frames had this latter feature), or fixed on brackets attached to the window uprights or wall. This trend of fixing shelves above the frame started when special block instruments – 'lock-and-block' instruments – were developed that were physically connected to certain levers, preventing signalmen pulling semaphore signals to 'all clear' if the line were already occupied by another train or before they had been authorised to do so by the signalman in the next signalbox to which the train was being sent.

Now comes the challenge for the modeller: how many block instruments and block bells (those ubiquitous rectangular boxes) need to be displayed on that cupboard or shelf to be authentic, and what should they look like? The fundamental questions are reasonably simple:

How many through lines does your signalbox control?
With how many signalboxes does your signalbox communicate?

Starting with the block bells, there should be one for communicating with every signalbox sending trains to and receiving trains from your signalbox, whether along single or double track, with one additional bell for every additional single or double line between signalboxes. Although the designs varied, block bells always incorporated a bell or spiral gong that was sounded by the actions of the signalman in the adjacent box. These bells and gongs were usually exposed on top of the wooden cases containing the electrical coils etc, so that they could be heard distinctly – and the brass lovingly polished by the signalmen. The most notable exception to this arrangement was adopted by the GNR, which used instruments with the bells hung underneath the wooden cases, so hidden that no signalman could reach under to polish them.

The majority of block bells also incorporated a Morse-key-type tapper that was used to activate the bell or gong in the adjacent signalbox. Companies using Sykes 'lock and block', Preece or Tyer's block instruments (see below) were supplied with separate plungers to do the job of the tappers.

Turning next to block instruments and ignoring the 'lock-and-block' variety for the moment, the feature that did not change over the years (and still remains true today where block working is in use) was the relationship of the number of indicators to a through train's direction of travel. Once you have understood this relationship every block instrument – irrespective of style or the railway company using it – will make sense, just as the fundamental principles of how many firebox holes a steam locomotive has does not change despite the huge variety of designs.

With block instruments there is always one indicator for trains approaching the signalbox and one for trains moving away from it. The former is operated by your signalman and forms part of what is often referred to as the 'pegging' instrument, while the latter – the 'non-pegging' instrument – is operated by the signalman to whom your signalman is sending the train. Those indicators could be single needles, miniature semaphores or 'flags' with words on them.

Therefore, if your signalbox controls trains at the terminus of a stretch of double track, for example, there should be just two indicators. It does not matter how complicated the track layout is at that terminus nor how many points/turnouts or signals; the number of block indicators remains the same – one for trains approaching the terminus, and one for trains departing from it [**117**].

If your signalbox controls trains passing in opposite directions over a stretch of double track there should be four indicators. The same arrangement could be found in many pre-World War 1 signalboxes controlling through trains on a single line (a practice that was effectively obsolete by the Grouping of 1923).

Sometimes each indicator was in a separate wooden case; sometimes the two indicators for trains travelling to and from

RIGHT ABOVE The long-obsolete practice of positioning block instruments on a shelf at the back of the signalbox – and opposite the lever frame – remained a feature of the LNWR's Carlisle No 5 signalbox until it closed in 1951. *BR(LMR)*

RIGHT BELOW Not the sharpest of photographs, but included to show that despite the number of levers in the GNR's signalbox at Skegness, because the terminal station was at the end of a simple section of double track, only two indicating block instruments were necessary. It is important to remember that the size of the signalbox and its lever frame has no direct bearing on the number of block instruments. *Nevis*

116

117

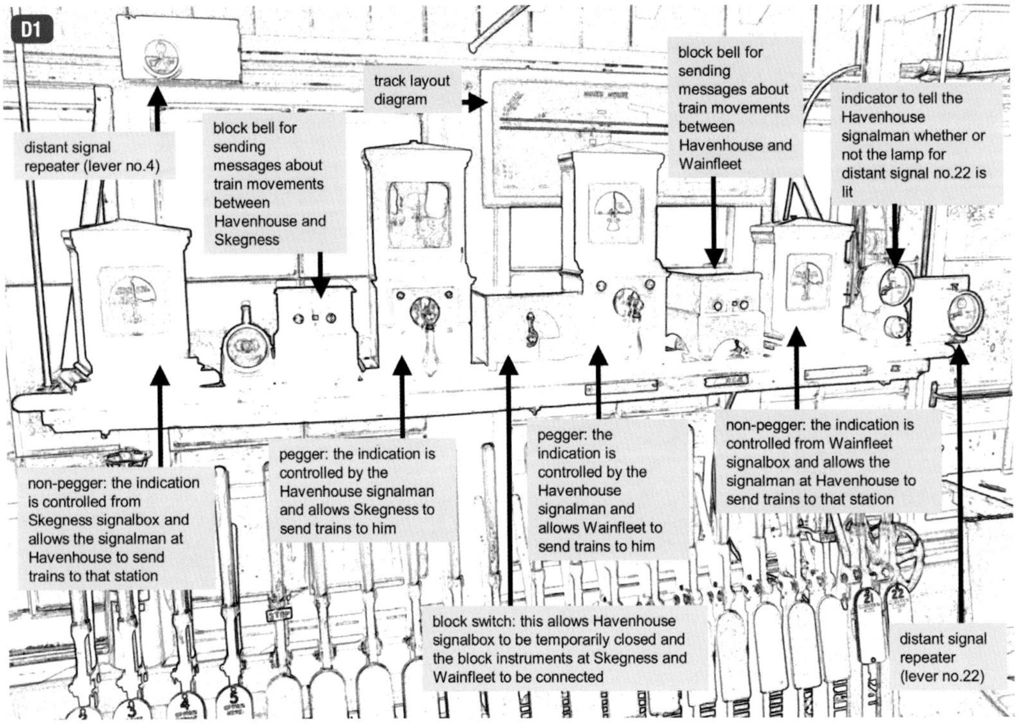

ABOVE A typical block shelf with four single-indication block instruments and two block bells for controlling a section of double track. Only the presence of two short block instruments (the non-peggers) and block bells with hidden bells betray this as a GNR block shelf – in this case inside Havenhouse signalbox. *Author*

LEFT The Havenhouse block shelf explained.

119

ABOVE The passage of trains over the section of double track controlled from the SER's Shalford signalbox was regulated using Walker's block instruments – the two largest rectangular boxes on the block shelf. Notice the Walker's plunger boxes immediately below each instrument. The row of track-circuit indicators above the row of signal repeaters was an SR addition (as were the lever-description plates). *BR(SR)*

the same signalbox were combined in one case. One of the earliest instruments made specifically for controlling the movement of trains between 'signal stations' was designed by C. V. Walker of the SER in the 1850s. It featured two miniature semaphores on the same post, the right-hand one activated by your signalman to tell his colleague he could send a train (the equivalent of the 'pegging' indication), the left-hand one operated by that distant signalman to indicate that he was prepared to accept a train (the equivalent of the 'non-pegging' indication) [*see* **119**].

Combining the indicators for trains travelling between adjacent signalboxes became a standard feature of instruments made by Tyer & Co from the early 1870s and then from the beginning of the 20th century in the designs of progressive railway companies, to save space on block shelves. The almost universal arrangement in these instruments was to align the indicators vertically with the 'pegging' one beneath the 'non-pegging' one, whether they were miniature semaphores, needles or flags.

To sum up, the block shelf (or cupboard) in a signalbox controlling a section of double track with trains passing in opposite directions will feature either four single-indicator or two double-indicator block instruments. The total number of indications will always be four – no more, no fewer.

Continuing with the double-track example but bringing the block bells into the equation, you could model the following permutations:

> two 'pegging' and two 'non-pegging' block instruments (each with one indicator) and two block bells [**118**, **Diagram 1**], or
>
> two block instruments (each with two indicators and the ability to 'peg' the lower of those indications) and two block bells.

If you have decided to model the interior of an SER signalbox with Walker's double-semaphore instruments, because each instrument sported its own block bell you will have just two instruments on the shelf, each with a small box beneath sporting the bell plunger and knob to change the indications of the miniature semaphore [**119**].

Block instruments developed by William Preece after 1862 were used extensively by the LSWR [**120**] and remained in use on BR until the 1970s. The accompanying diagrams show a block shelf of these instruments for controlling a double section of track compared with instruments patented by Spagnoletti in 1862 for exactly the same purpose [*see* **112**] and used by the GWR and BR for a similarly long period [**Diagrams 2 and 3**].

120

ABOVE The block shelf inside the LSWR's Fulwell Junction signalbox, equipped with block instruments designed by William Preece. Because the signalbox communicates with three adjacent signalboxes there are three indicating block instruments (with the miniature semaphores), each with its 'pegging' switch handles (miniature levers) to its left. Although six plungers are visible, only three were used to communicate with the three adjacent signalboxes. *Dr J. W. F. Scrimgeour/ Kidderminster Railway Museum (SE175/1)*

D2

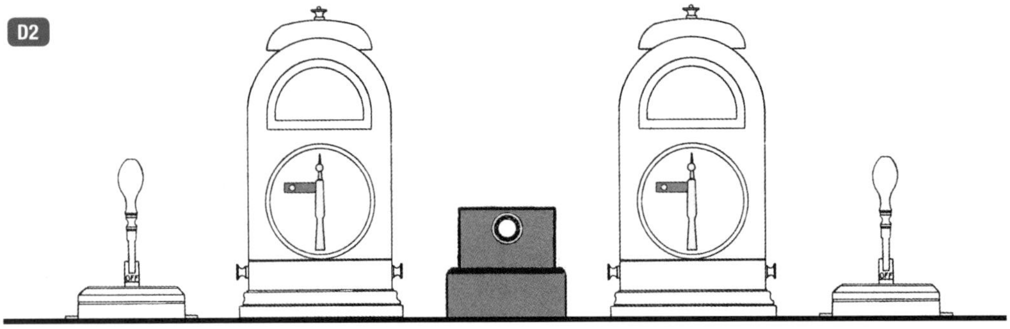

ABOVE The arrangement of Preece block instruments and bells used to control a section of double track on LSWR lines. The lollipop-shaped objects are miniature levers, the equivalent of the 'commutator' or operating handle on a pegging block instrument.

Another combination of instruments you might choose to model was marketed by Tyer & Co, a favoured supplier of electrical equipment to many railway companies from the late 1860s until well into the 20th century. For controlling trains between adjacent signalboxes it supplied all the necessary instruments attached to one vertical board. These boards of instruments were first developed so they could be attached to the wall of a signalbox, but increasingly from the 1880s they were hung over the lever frame. The standard distribution of instruments on these boards was, from top to bottom, a bell or gong, a two-indicator block instrument (either miniature semaphores, favoured by the LBSCR [**121**], or needles, favoured by the GER) and a plunger (although in some varieties this was incorporated into the main instrument case). To control that ubiquitous section of double track a signalbox would have been fitted with just two boards of instruments [**Diagram 4**].

At the beginning of the 20th century Tyer & Co produced new instruments which, by virtue of having the indicators, bell or gong and tapper or plunger fitted into one very large (and heavy) wooden case, dispensed with the board altogether [**Diagram 5**]. The firm was responding to a trend that appears to have started with the LNWR

D3

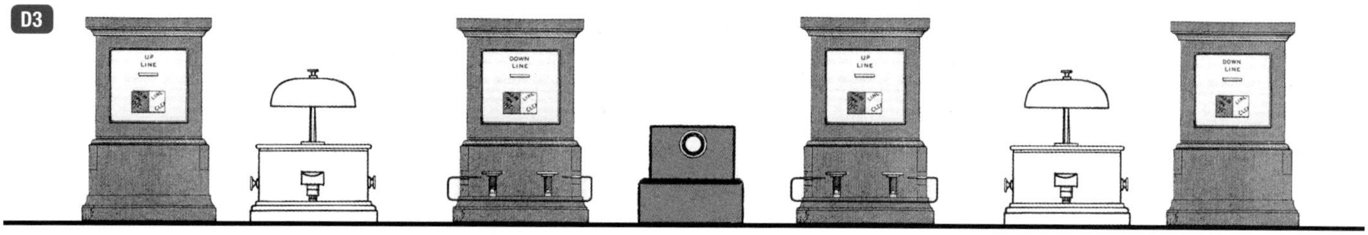

121

ABOVE The arrangement of Spagnoletti block instruments and bells used to control a section of double track on GWR lines.

LEFT Typical arrangement of Tyer's block instruments in an LBSCR signalbox controlling trains passing on a section of double track. *Author's collection*

BELOW The arrangement of Tyer's instruments used to control a section of double track on LBSCR lines.

D4

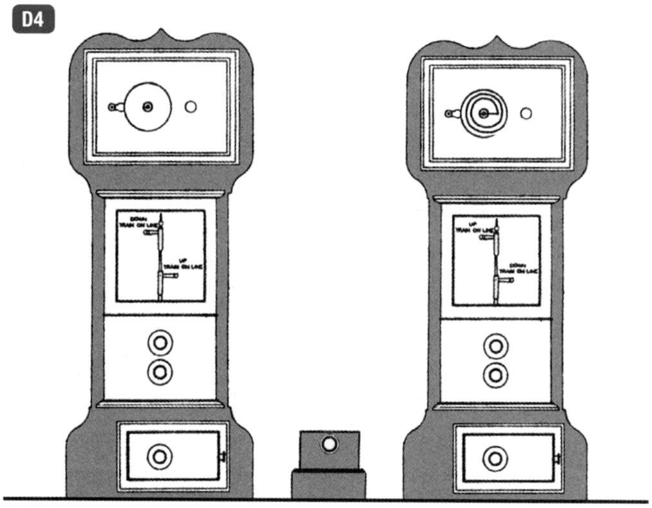

when it produced its own 'combined' instrument at the end of the 1880s. Where such instruments were used to control a double-track section of line only two were required – in modelling terms, only two rectangular boxes need to appear on your block shelf [**Diagram 6**]. Other companies developed their own 'combined' instruments, Tyer's had produced another two variants by nationalisation [**122**], and nowadays, in the second decade of the 21st century, all block instruments still in use conform to this 'combined' standard, although they are of the modular design developed in the 1950s for BR's London Midland Region [*see* **124**].

Assuming you have stayed the course thus far and all has made sense, let us now be more adventurous and add a double-line junction to our section of double track. In this scenario your signalbox will be communicating with not two but three other signalboxes. Consequently, the arrangement of instruments on your block shelf (or cupboard) could be one of the following:

- three 'pegging' and three 'non-pegging' block instruments (each with one indicator) and three block bells
- three block instruments (each with two indicators and the ability to 'peg' one of those indications) and three block bells
- three 'combined' block instruments (each with two indicators and the ability to 'peg' one of those indications and block bell).

Those of you who have remembered what was stated previously about the number of indicators and bells needed in block working will have realised that the three examples above are not the only combinations you could have at this double-line junction. You could have a mixture of single- or double-indicator instruments with separate bells, as well as one or more 'combined' instruments, etc etc, as long as the total number of indicators is never greater or less than six, and the total number of bells never greater or less than three. To repeat the rule, there should always be one indicator for trains approaching the signalbox and one for trains moving away from it, along with a bell for communicating with every signalbox sending trains to and receiving trains from your signalbox, plus one additional bell for every additional single or double line between signalboxes.

Permissive Block instruments

Brief mention can now be made of special variants of block instrument that were devised to control trains on goods lines using Permissive Block regulations. Not all railway companies used these special instruments, the GNR, for example, using the same design of block instruments for either Absolute or Permissive working. On lines where permissive working was authorised, more than one train was allowed to occupy the section of track between signalboxes. Special instruments were therefore devised, not only to display the standard indications of 'normal', 'line clear' or 'train on line' but also to indicate the number of trains in a section. Until nationalisation Tyer & Co supplied most of the instruments used for this purpose, although the LMS adopted the LNWR's own design. If on a GWR layout you have goods or slow lines in addition to through main

122

LEFT The block instruments seen in this 1950s photograph of the ex-CR signalbox at Symington were examples of one of the last new designs marketed by Tyer & Co. Each was 480mm high, 290mm wide and 240mm deep. *Author's collection*

RIGHT Part of the block shelf inside Hereford Brecon Curve signalbox. The large instruments with sloping fronts are Tyer's permissive instruments, the smaller ones made to Spagnoletti's 1863 patent. *Dr J. W. F. Scrimgeour/ Kidderminster Railway Museum (SE194/1)*

D5

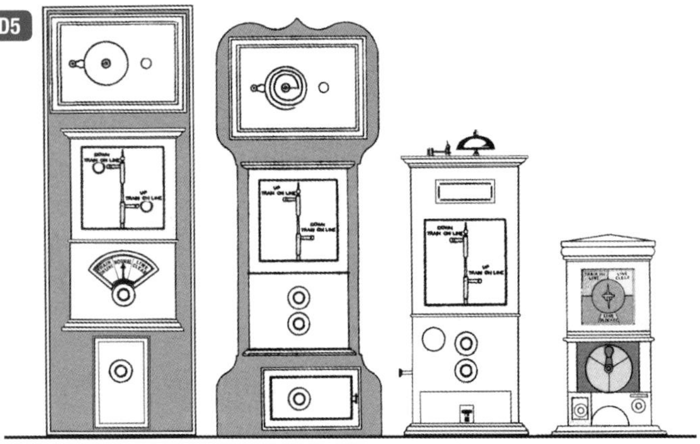

ABOVE The relative sizes of three Tyer's block instruments compared to an MR rotary instrument on the far right. From left to right the instruments were used by the GSWR, LBSCR and CR.

D6

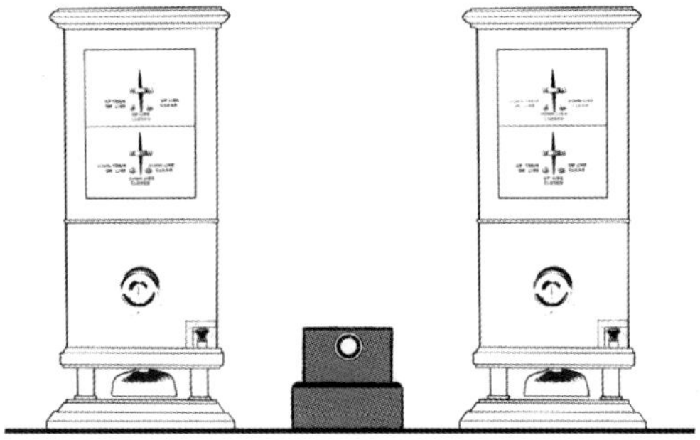

ABOVE The arrangement of LNWR block instruments used to control a section of double track on that company's lines.

lines, then because the difference in appearance of Tyer's Permissive instruments and standard Spagnoletti patent block instruments was so marked it will be worth the effort of modelling them on your block shelf [**123**]. By contrast, if you model a stretch of the MR (i.e. pre-1923) with goods lines you will not need to portray any goods-line instruments at all, as that company did not use them (signalmen communicating by block bell). After 1923 the LMS remedied this omission by progressively introducing the LNWR style of instruments – which, because of their size difference from standard MR single-indication instruments, would be conspicuous by their absence if not modelled [*see* **112**].

After nationalisation two other designs of Permissive instrument made their appearance, one confined to former GWR lines, the other conforming to the same modular design as its Absolute partner and intended to become the standard instrument for goods-line control [**124**, **Diagram 7**].

Lock-and-block instruments

We turn now to the perplexing subject of 'lock and block'. Although there were a number of patented arrangements in the Victorian period, from a modelling point of view there are only two common forms worth considering, both of which survived in use into the 1980s. The first were instruments made to William Sykes patents and used by a number of companies on their commuter lines, the majority of installations being in and around London on routes operated by the LBSCR, SER, LCDR, LSWR and GER. Sykes instruments were also installed by the Hull & Barnsley and Lancashire, Derbyshire & East Coast railways and in a few locations on the LTSR, GSWR and NBR. The second-most-extensively used 'lock-and-block' variant was the so-called 'rotary block' designed and used by the MR on many of its main lines and at certain other important locations.

123

The rule about the number of block bells stated above also applies where 'lock-and-block' working is in operation, so at least that is one less complication for the modeller.

The familiar Sykes arrangement appeared after William Sykes obtained his 1880 patent (No 1907) following experimentation in the previous decade. In its simplest form only one instrument (with associated block bell and plunger) was required to regulate the passage of trains between adjacent signalboxes. This meant that in a signalbox controlling a section of double track there would be two instruments, two block bells and two bell plungers. In many SR signalboxes the block bells were fixed to boards suspended above and at 90° to the block shelf (another effective way of obscuring a signalman's view outside).

A basic Sykes 'lock-and-block' instrument, in its simplest form, consisted of a rectangular wooden case above which was attached a cylindrical, glazed metal case containing a miniature semaphore. In the wooden case there was a circular glazed aperture behind which were two slots, the lower either blank or displaying the words 'TRAIN ON', the upper displaying either 'LOCKED' or 'FREE'. Beneath this aperture were a brass plunger and a hook (the 'switch hook') that was arranged to fit over it. (It is not useful here to go into how Sykes instruments were operated; any modeller interested should consult more specialist books on signalling.)

Although on reading this description the simplest form of Sykes instrument appears to be completely different to other block instruments, a comparison can be made. The miniature semaphore and the upper slot of the aperture in the main case are in effect the 'non-pegging' part of the sort of 'combined' block instrument considered earlier, the lower slot, the plunger and its associated switch hook being equivalent to the 'pegging' part.

If, in addition to the signal controlling entry to the next section, there was another home signal which it was felt necessary to include as part of the 'lock and block' arrangement, the configuration of instruments would be as shown in the accompanying diagram [**125**, **Diagram 8**].

There is no doubt that trying to model Sykes equipment authentically is difficult, and many might consider it not worth the effort. It is certainly much easier to model the MR's 'rotary block' equipment because, visually, this differed in only one respect from the standard, single-indication units we have examined already. In the 'pegging' instrument there was a very prominent brass disc and stubby handle on the front of the lower section [*see* **108**, **112**]; in 4mm-gauge modelling this would be a blob of paint a little under 2mm in diameter. The accompanying diagram shows the distribution of instruments on a typical block shelf controlling trains on a stretch of double track [**Diagram 9**]. In some locations the rotary ('pegging') and non-pegging instruments were interposed, thereby putting extra distance between the two rotary instruments for opposite lines, presumably to reduce the risk of a signalman's operating the wrong instrument.

D7

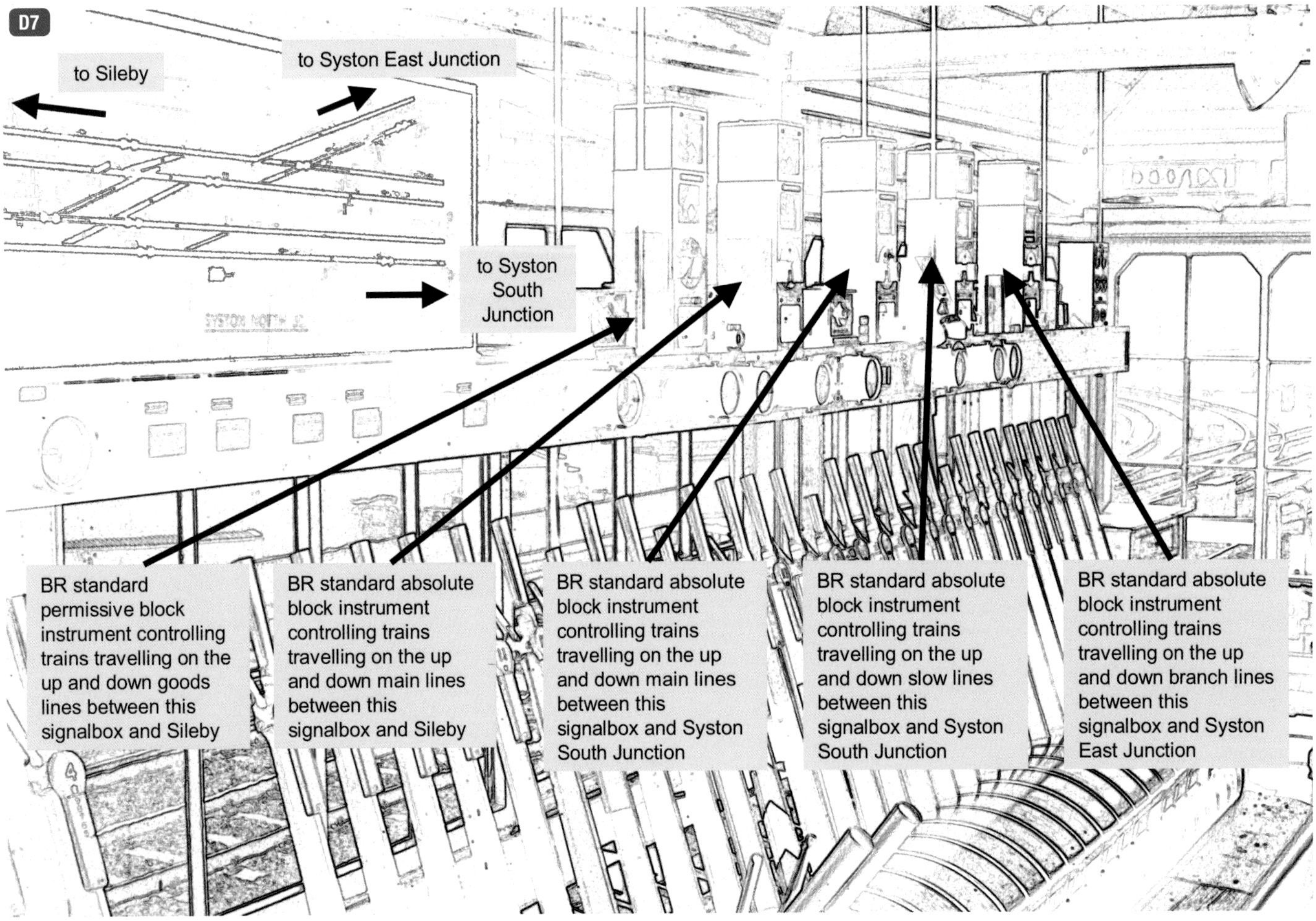

124

ABOVE An explanation of the relationship between the track layout at Syston North Junction and the block instruments.

RIGHT Part of the interior of the MR signalbox at Syston North Junction, photographed in 1984 and featuring block instruments of standard BR modular design. *Author*

Dimensions of block instruments

As it is almost impossible to find any historical or secondary sources giving the sizes of electrical signalbox equipment (and having been critical of the miscellaneous array of rectangular boxes on model block shelves), this author felt it would be useful to list the basic dimensions of the main block instruments mentioned so far. The list is not exhaustive, but all the most common instruments that you might want to re-create in model form are here. Apart from the BR standard 'domino' or 'plastic' instrument, which because of its modular nature had to be manufactured to precise dimensions, the sizes of all other instruments, the wooden cases for which were made individually by cabinet makers, could vary from those quoted by a maximum of plus or minus 25mm.

Other electrical equipment

Having examined Absolute, Permissive and lock-and-block instruments we can now look at other electrical equipment that might legitimately appear on your model block shelf. Remember the underlying principle that the earlier the date of your model, the less equipment needs to be portrayed. You will not need to fill your shelf with loads of extra rectangular boxes and dials until the 1930s.

As signalboxes began to proliferate, from the 1870s, companies were keen not to have all of them open all the time. Therefore, to allow a signalbox to be closed temporarily and the block instruments of adjacent signalboxes connected together to maintain communication, the wiring was routed through a 'closing' or 'block switch'. (Although the design of block switches varied, so as to give modellers an idea of the relative sizes of block instruments, all the diagrams in this chapter show a generic representation of the same block switch approximately 150mm wide by 140mm high.)

The next instrument to find its way onto block shelves was the signal repeater. Where signals were visible from signalboxes, signalmen were expected to look to make sure that they had responded correctly to the appropriate lever, but where important

DIMENSIONS OF BLOCK INSTRUMENTS				
ITEM	**Height**	**Width**	**Depth**	**Notes**
Typical single-indication (always a needle) instrument used in both pegging and non-pegging forms [see 118]	475mm	205mm	95mm (upper section) 150mm (lower section)	Although details varied, instruments of these dimensions were widely used by all pre-Grouping companies at some time, and they became standard block instruments on the GNR, MR, MSLR/GCR, NBR and NER. After the Welwyn accident of 1935 on the LNER, pegging instruments used on the main line were fitted with an extra box on the back to cover additional, electrical contacts.
MR rotary (pegging)	475mm	205mm	140mm (upper section) 180mm (lower section)	
MR block bell case (excluding the height of any bell)	130mm	205mm (base 230mm)	230mm (base 255mm)	
GWR Spagnoletti (single-indication, pegging and non-pegging)	305mm	190mm (lower section) 170mm (upper section)	120mm (lower section) 90mm (upper section)	
GWR Spagnoletti i.e. pegging and (double-indication, non-pegging combined)	380mm	190mm (lower section) 170mm (upper section)	120mm (lower section) 90mm (upper section)	Later instruments were fitted with an extra box on the back to cover additional, electrical contacts.
GWR '1947' combined	410mm	170mm	175mm	
GWR block bell case (excluding the height of any bell)	110mm	150mm (base 190mm)	235mm (base 270mm)	These are the dimensions of what became the standard block bell which superseded other Victorian examples of various measurements.
Sykes 'lock and block'	360mm	205mm	150mm	With the cylindrical case for the miniature semaphore added, the overall height of the instrument could be 580mm.
Tyer's double-indication (either miniature semaphores or needles)	470mm	240mm	140mm	Instruments of these dimensions were supplied to the GER, LBSCR, CR, GSWR and NSR.
Tyer's block bell/gong (case excluding any bell or gong)	205mm (base 255mm)	290mm (base 310mm)	120mm	These are the dimensions when the unit is viewed attached to a backboard; to compare the dimensions directly with a MR bell, for example, although the width remains the same, the height and depth measurements need to be transposed.
Tyer's plunger	110mm (base 150mm)	205mm (base 240mm)	90mm	
Tyer's board as supplied to the LBSCR on which a double indication instrument, bell/gong and plunger were attached	990mm	290mm (min) 390mm (max)	20mm	
Tyer's board as supplied to the GSWR on which a double indication instrument, bell/gong and plunger were attached	1,070mm	375mm	25mm	
Tyer's double-indication instrument (1902 and 1919 patents)	510mm	250mm	140mm	The NSR was the main user of 1902 patent instruments; 1919 1919 patents) patent were supplied to the LBSCR and lines in Ireland.
Tyer's board as supplied for the 1902 and 1919 patent instruments and bell/gong	830mm	380mm	25mm	
Tyer's Permissive Block instrument (single-indicator variety)	500mm	240mm	150mm) (lower section – tapering to 100mm at the top of the upper section	
Preece single miniature semaphore	390mm (to top of arch)	205mm	230mm	
Walker's double miniature semaphore	395mm (excluding bell)	280mm	255mm	
BR standard modular design ('domino' or 'plastic block')	128mm (i.e. exactly 5in)	152mm (i.e. exactly 6in)	152mm (i.e. exactly 6in)	These are the dimensions of individual modules that could house a needle indication, commutator ('pegging' mechanism) or bell and tapper. For controlling a section of double track between signalboxes, a 'standard' instrument would be made up of four modules stacked vertically – i.e. two indicators, commutator, bell and tapper. [see 124]
GNR block bell (large case)	200mm	230mm (top section) 240mm (lower section)	230mm (top section) 240mm (lower section)	
GNR block bell (small case)	180mm	165mm (top section) 175mm (lower section)	230mm (top section) 240mm (lower section)	

These dimensions ignore decorative moulding details, including the prominent 'pediments' on the typical single-needle block instruments and on Tyer's permissive instruments, for example.

D9

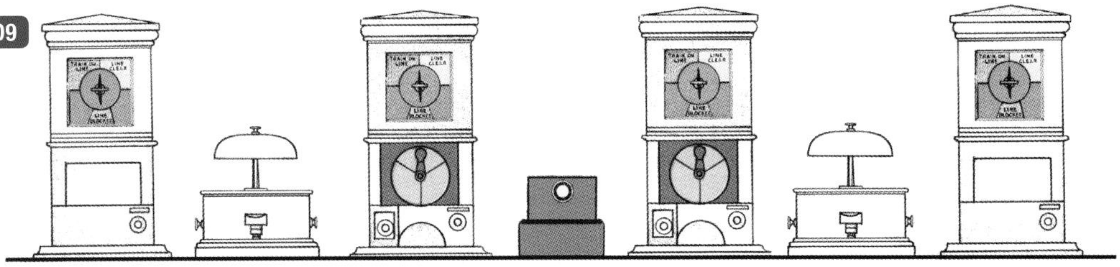

LEFT The arrangement of MR block instruments (including two rotary 'lock and block' instruments) and bells used to control a section of double track. Note that, apart from the style of instrument, the arrangement is the same as for the GNR's Havenhouse block shelf [*see* **118**].

125

ABOVE Some of the Sykes 'lock and block' instruments in the LSWR's Shacklegate Junction signalbox. The instrument on the right is for accepting trains on the branch from Fulwell Junction; the two on the left illustrate the standard arrangement for controlling trains passing through in just one direction on a section of double track – in this particular location, from Strawberry Hill to Teddington. Out of sight at the other end of the block shelf was a similar arrangement of instruments for controlling trains travelling from Teddington to Strawberry Hill. *Dr J. W. F. Scrimgeour/ Kidderminster Railway Museum (SE332/2)*

D8

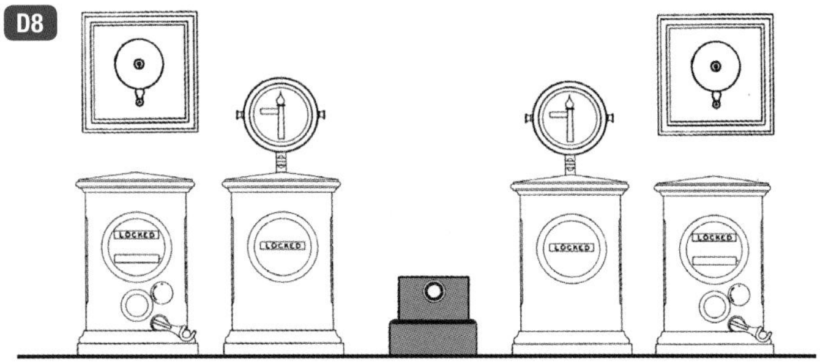

ABOVE The arrangement of Sykes 'lock and block' instruments and bells used to control a section of double track where home and starting signals were 'locked/ unlocked' by the actions of the signalmen in the adjacent signalboxes.

signals were hidden from view, signal repeaters were installed (albeit often with some reluctance on the part of the railway company). The indications of these instruments could take the form of miniature semaphores or single needles. Most early examples were housed in wooden cases, many surviving in use well into the 20th century (and on preserved railways still), but the design that became most popular in the 20th century was the cylindrical glazed brass (and then finally plastic) container. In Victorian-era signalboxes the wooden-cased variety were often positioned behind the levers operating the signals for which they displayed the indications. In the 20th century it was more usual to find them fixed to block shelves positioned above the appropriate lever; this was particularly so with the cylindrical variety. As some railway companies began to install more and more of the latter they altered the design of their block shelves to accommodate them, fitting either a vertical board along the back edge or the equivalent of a pelmet along the front edge, onto which the instruments could be attached. In extreme cases another shelf immediately above the block shelf was installed to accommodate repeaters, probably the most impressive example being in the GWR's Reading Main Line West signalbox, where there was an almost continuous extra shelf running the full length of the 198-lever frame. By the 1930s it was also common in SR signalboxes to find that the boards on which the block bells were fixed above the block shelves additionally supported an array of signal repeaters with enamel numbers indicating the levers to which they referred. After World War 2 it became increasingly common in main-line signalboxes to repeat electrically the indications of all the running-line signals.

Certain varieties of signal repeater were also made that could indicate whether or not a semaphore's lamp was alight, some incorporating a bell to give signalmen an audible warning if a light had been extinguished. Also available were instruments that indicated only the state of the signal lights; these were commonly referred to as lamp repeaters and could be wired up to a single semaphore or a group of signals. Following the widespread introduction of colour-light signals after World War 2 it became more usual to repeat their indications in signalboxes using appropriately coloured lights [*see* **113**]. Like their needle or miniature-semaphore counterparts they were positioned above or close to the relevant lever.

Occasionally electrical indicators were used to show whether or not a point/turnout had responded correctly to the operation of a mechanical lever, but these were never commonplace. Motor-worked points/turnouts, however, would always be connected to a repeater in the signalbox, the standard by BR days being a pair of lights displaying either 'N' for normal or 'R' for reversed.

As track circuiting made its appearance at the end of the 19th century, repeaters with centrally pivoted horizontal flags or 'banners' came into use. When the track was occupied the banner would be horizontal, the word 'OCCUPIED' usually being visible; when it was clear the banner would be inclined at 45°, usually exposing 'CLEAR' [*see* **102**, **111**]. At locations where more than a handful of track circuits were installed, illuminated track diagrams – so called because they incorporated small electric bulbs to indicate whether or not certain stretches of track were occupied – became the preferred alternative to cluttering the block shelf with rows of individual

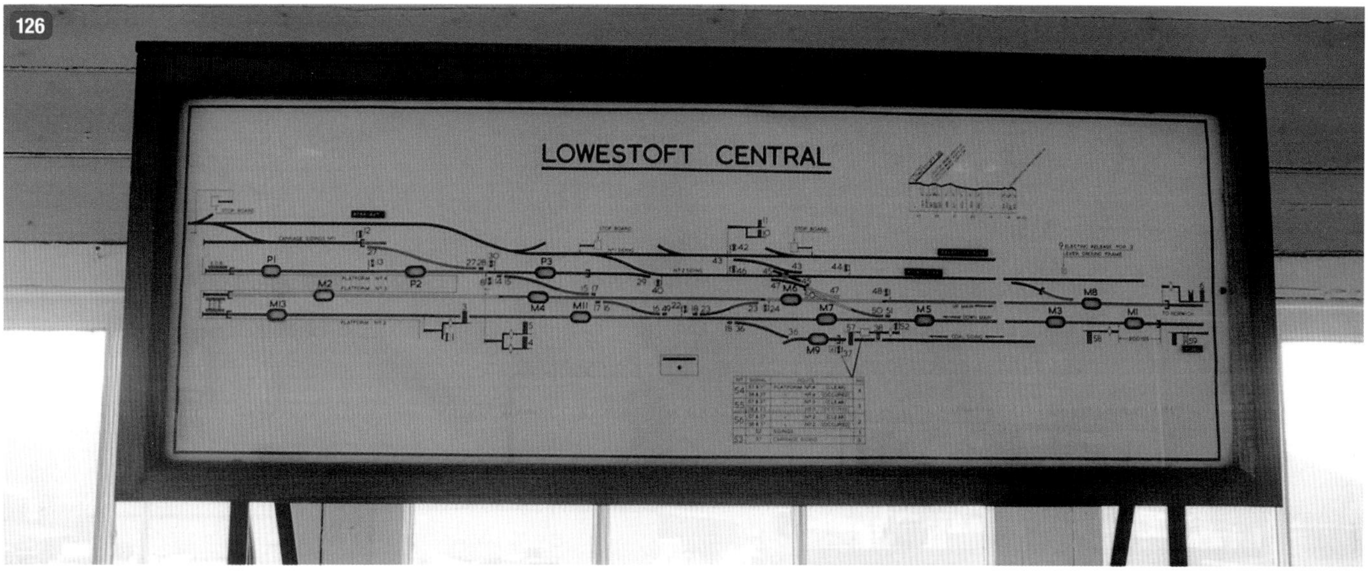

ABOVE A typical BR(ER) illuminated diagram, photographed inside Lowestoft signalbox in 1996. *Author*

repeaters. When illuminated diagrams first appeared just before World War 1 the norm was for the bulbs to be illuminated unless the track were occupied, but as this could consume a lot of battery power (what would those thrifty Victorian managers have thought?) the reverse became standard during the 1930s [**126**]. Other than on the country's principal main lines, however, illuminated diagrams did not find their way into every signalbox, so the individual track-circuit indicator was never completely superseded.

Over the years there were, of course, other items of specialist electrical instrument that could be found on a block shelf – train-platform indicators, plungers to sound bells on platforms, block-instrument releases and train describers. The last-mentioned were far less common than block instruments and confined to busy signalboxes where it was important signalmen should know where trains were coming from and going to over a variety of routes. Modellers who wish to know more about other instruments are recommended to seek out specialist signalling books.

Single-line instruments

The one piece of signalling equipment you certainly would not have found on a block shelf was a single-line instrument. As stated at the beginning of this chapter, until just before World War 1 the cupboards or block shelves of signalboxes on single-track branches sported block instruments almost identical to those regulating trains on double-track sections. The only other visible sign of single-line control you could reproduce in model form, as well as those standard block instruments, would be a signalman handing a staff (or other token in a pouch at the end of a metal hoop) to the locomotive crew, or vice versa. It was not until after 1878, when Edward Tyer patented his first electrical single-line device, that additional rectangular shapes, used for issuing and receiving metal tokens to be used in place of the staff, began to appear in signalboxes. The Board of Trade was initially unconvinced about Tyer's new device (nor subsequent improvements) [**127**] and continued to insist upon block instruments or the continued use of staffs. In fact it was this reluctance to approve token working that led F. W. Webb and A. M. Thompson of the LNWR to design and patent (in 1889) an electrical machine for issuing and receiving

BELOW An example of a Tyer's No 6 single-line-tablet instrument, in use inside the North Yorkshire Moors Railway's Grosmont signalbox. *Author*

128

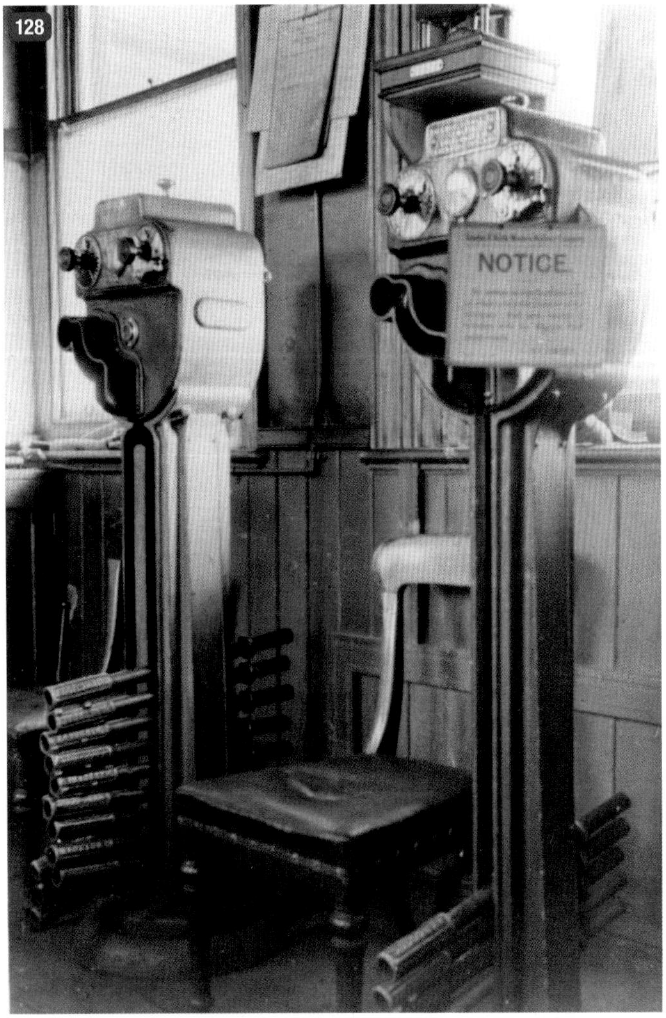

ABOVE Webb & Thompson's electric staff instruments came in a number of subtly different varieties, two of which are shown here at the LNWR's Rotton Park Road station – one with two slots for holding the staffs, the other with just one. *W. A. Camwell*

129

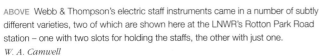

ABOVE An example of a Tyer's No 9 single-line-key-token instrument, preserved in the GWR signalbox at Fencote. These instruments were developed on the GWR and then made and marketed by Tyer & Co after World War 1. *Author*

staffs, the company allowing the Railway Signal Co to manufacture it under licence for use by other railways [**128**].

If you are modelling the interior of a signalbox controlling a single-track line post-1923 you can safely do without block instruments, but you must include one of the many manifestations of Tyer's instrument [**129**], the distinctive cast-iron tower of Webb & Thompson's instrument or its miniature version. Irrespective of type, these were much larger than any block instrument, and even if you have decided not to bother modelling the latter, the absence of a single-line instrument, often painted green or red, inside your single-line-branch signalbox might be considered a serious omission [*see* **77**].

Photographs reveal that although there was no absolute convention as to where these devices were positioned inside the signalbox, many were very visible from the outside. They could be located at the ends of the lever frame, against the back wall or sometimes next to an end wall. You would not be criticised for any of those positions and so have the excuse, if you like to show off your modelling skills, to use a prominent window position.

Part 3 Altogether now

By the end of the 1930s the LNER was leading the way with progressive resignalling projects, and a fundamental change was taking place that is now at the heart of all modern signalling installations. This was the physical bringing together inside signalboxes of all the functions previously performed separately by mechanical and electrical means. Switches activated colour-light signals or motor-worked points/turnouts, lights told the signalman whether or not he had responded correctly to the turning of those switches, and all were brought together with the illuminated diagram incorporating the track-circuit indicators.

There were two manifestations of the new arrangement, these being the OCS ('one control switch') and NX ('entrance/exit') panels. The standard appearance of the former was with switches arranged in a sloping facia along the bottom of the diagram [**130**]; in the latter, switches or buttons were embedded in the appropriate tracks on the diagram. It need not concern us here how these panels worked or how they were operated; again, specialist signalling books will fulfil a modeller's curiosity.

Panels were not the automatic choice for new or resignalling projects until the 1960s. Even then, new or reclaimed mechanical frames of both full-size and miniature levers were still being installed, usually in isolated 'like-for-like' situations, whereas OCS or NX panels were chosen for more extensive projects. By the 1970s, however, when mechanical installations were no longer an option, the NX panel became the standard for any new or replacement signalling work.

Ironically, given their electrical and electronic complexity, panels are easier to model than are fiddly levers, which need painting and setting at convincing angles, and rows of rectangular boxes on precarious block shelves. Unfortunately the comparative simplicity of modelling panels is of little or no benefit if you are authentically reproducing most styles of powerboxes in the period from 1960 to the end of the 1980s, for the view inside will be restricted by a large overhanging roof (fitted in real life to prevent direct sunlight falling on the illuminated panel [*see* **16**]) or by windows – usually fitted with blinds – that are too small to see through.

The final development in railway signalling is worth knowing about because, although the new equipment could be (and in some locations was) housed in buildings with no windows, it also found its way into structures with lots of glass, providing great views out for the operating staff – and, consequently, great views in for the modeller. The late 1980s witnessed the elimination of the illuminated diagram and the transfer of all information onto one or more computer screen. Signalmen (and women) became 'signallers', and for the first time in more than a century they spent the majority of their shifts sitting in comfortable chairs in eerily quiet office-type surroundings, occasionally tapping on a computer keyboard or manipulating a 'tracker ball' as trains were automatically routed according to a national, computerised timetable. The signaller's job became more like that of an air-traffic controller, though with far less contact with crews. The internal layout of these 'signalling centres' depends on the number of discrete areas being controlled, each usually being allocated its own 'workstation'. From a modelling point of view these workstations look like large desks with a bank of screens at which just one signaller is seated.

BELOW The OCS panel that was installed in the new signalbox at Huddersfield in 1958. *BR(LMR)*

130

Part 4 Everything else

Heating

Arguably the most important item inside a signalbox after the equipment for controlling trains was (and remains) the means of heating the operating room. Until the end of the 19th century the open fire (burning coal, of course) was the most common form in both wooden and brick/stone-built signalboxes. Either in the back wall or a corner of the structure, a standard chimney of brick would be constructed with a domestic-style cast-iron hob grate or in some signalboxes a small range (i.e. with oven). There was nothing unusual in the way in which the chimney and hearth were formed in a signalbox; they were built exactly as single-flue chimneys would have been in any other structure.

In signalboxes with no lower storey, such as Saxby's early cabins on stilts or structures on metal frameworks spanning the tracks, cast-iron stoves had to be used, and by the middle of the 20th century these had also found their way into all other types of signalbox. In many, stoves were fitted into the original open fireplaces, the hot gases and smoke being piped into the existing brick chimney [**131**]. In other structures the open fire might simply be blocked up and the stove fitted in another location, or, more drastically, the whole chimney might be removed before the stove was fitted in its place. In very long signalboxes there were often two stoves.

At the beginning of the 20th century central heating was no longer a novelty in domestic architecture, albeit still confined to city properties or the grand country homes of wealthy businessmen. Obviously, central heating was an option only where there was access to a supply of gas or electricity, and signalboxes at large railway centres where the first to benefit [**132**].

Electric heating, in line with its adoption in the wider community, became viable in signalboxes only after World War 2 when the National Grid was extended to reach most parts of the country. Many new signalboxes of the 1950s were equipped with electric radiators, and this form of heating became the norm in all subsequent new powerboxes. But, for the majority of mechanical signalboxes, until very recently coal fires were still the most common form of heating.

ABOVE An interior view of the GER's signalbox at Lowestoft, recorded in 1996, illustrates the progression of heating methods from the original open fire – boarded up so that a cast-iron stove could be installed – to the suspiciously small domestic electric heater. *Author*

In many locations open fires lasted longer than might be expected, and in the 1980s, by which time central heating had become a domestic necessity, it was still possible to find signalmen shovelling coal into stoves in signalboxes all over the country.

Furniture

Until well into the 20th century traditional mechanical signalboxes were provided with very little furniture. Probably the most important items were the clock and the wooden desk or writing slope. On the latter the train register, in which the times of all communications via the block instruments were recorded, would always have been open, and if you are going to the trouble of modelling a signalbox interior accurately you must never omit the clock or this vital book; the two are inseparable. Some pre-Grouping companies preferred to equip their signalboxes with free-standing desks; others placed a writing slope on cupboards or attached it to a wall. But there was always a special area for keeping the train register up to date.

Notice boards were invariably provided so that the special regulations and bell codes specific to that signalbox could be displayed along with amendments to the Rule Book, the latest train workings, contact details and arrangements for fogmen etc. By the beginning of the 20th century, calendars were common and photographs from the Edwardian era show that coloured prints – not always of railway subjects – were also pinned up.

Cupboards were a feature of all signalboxes from the beginning. As stated above, before the 1880s block instruments were often fixed on top of the cupboards with the wet cell batteries inside. Little space was needed for anything else – cleaning materials, brushes, mops, dusters, etc. Any inflammable substances, such as lamp oil, would have been stored in outbuildings. In pre-Grouping days, when many signalboxes were manned on 12-hour shifts and the signalmen lived close by, there was little need to provide cupboards for personal items. Metal lockers for such items were a mid-20th-century addition at new, larger signalboxes where more than just one signalman per shift and other staff might be working.

Photographs of pre-Grouping signalbox interiors do show that some companies provided simple wooden chests that doubled as seating. Many companies supplied high stools, often with padded seats. Sometimes standard domestic chairs appear in photographs, but the ubiquitous tatty 'comfy' chair so familiar in signalboxes of the 1970s would not have been tolerated in the Victorian era; its presence would still have been a disciplinary matter between the wars, and its popularity and eventual acceptance by management was probably related to the loss of traffic on the railways in the 1960s and a reduction in the time a signalman spent on his feet pulling and pushing levers. Other 'luxury' items that began to creep into operating rooms in BR days were items such as Belfast sinks and small electric cookers.

Lighting

A vital fitting in all signalboxes without exception was lighting, and the type of illumination provided largely kept pace with developments in shops, offices and other workplaces. Oil lamps would have been standard at first, and, where available, gas lighting. The latter was improved enormously with the perfection of the mantle at the end of the 19th century, which also gave oil lamps a new lease of life, the final evolution being the Tilley and Aladdin paraffin lamps used as back-up lighting in many signalboxes well into the 1970s.

132

ABOVE A crowd of proud NER staff on a visit to one of the new Newcastle signalboxes of 1909. Both the electro-pneumatic frame of miniature levers and the cast-iron hot-water radiator (of which one member of the party seems particularly appreciative) would have been considered wonders of their age by most of the men present. *Author's collection*

When electricity was available, light fittings also conformed to the latest domestic and workplace standards – first the Edison bulb and then, by the 1960s, in new signalboxes and powerboxes, the fluorescent tube.

Now that it has become easier to install lighting on model railways, the immediate temptation is to illuminate the signalbox and thus show off all those internal fittings. But a word of warning: lighting in real-life signalboxes has always been provided so that the signalman can see what he was doing at night, not to shed light outside the signalbox. Indeed, in the Board of Trade 'requirements' attention was drawn to the dangers posed by locomotive crews mistaking for signals any lights that might be visible from signalboxes. Lamps were often directed to shine only on the vital areas of operation – the lever frame, track diagram, block instruments and train register. Therefore, in model form, if you wish your traditional mechanical signalbox to be authentic, the lighting inside should be of far less intensity than that in station buildings. Model mechanical signalboxes should not become lighthouses. The illumination in powerboxes and signalling centres was of 'office' standards, so models of them can have a more powerful glow.

People

Until World War 1 the person working a signalbox would always have been a man, and he would always have been in his company's uniform – trousers, shirt, tie, waistcoat, jacket and cap for outside use [*see* **63**, **95**]. He might or might not have been supplied with an overcoat. During World War 1 many women were trained to operate signalboxes, and they too would have appeared in company uniform. As the 20th century progressed, the wearing of the complete issue uniform seems, from photographic evidence, to have become more 'relaxed', so much so that by BR days only the older generation were seen in regulation dress, younger staff being in jumpers and 'open-necked' shirts.

If you are a 'people' person there are many good reasons for having more than one character in your signalbox. Large and/or busy signalboxes often had two signalmen on duty, as well as a telegraph lad seated by the telegraph instruments or telephones and train register. The new Waterloo signalbox of 1936 had three banks of miniature levers and was worked by four signalmen and two telegraph lads. The panels in many later powerboxes were divided up in a similar fashion, with a signalman in charge of each section.

Even if you model a small mechanical signalbox you can always find reasons for extra people. You might wish to show the fireman in his overalls, wiping his boots at the top of the signalbox steps before being allowed entry to sign the train register. Worse still, you could fill the operating floor with S&T staff. You could capture the moment shifts change, or how about a trainee signalman learning the job with the regular signalman, or that regular man sitting in a corner whilst the trainee is working the frame, closely watched by a (uniformed) inspector?

If your model is pre-World War 1 or of a country location up until World War 2 you might wish to show a wife, son or daughter bringing lunch or dinner to the signalbox. And as many who have experienced it first-hand will know, there is always an opportunity to include an unofficial visitor – the enthusiastic schoolboy 'learning the job'. Of course, you could also fill the place with people on a special visit [*see* **132**], and a school party might usefully obscure other, more difficult items to model, such as the levers and block instruments!

5 The Finishing Touches

If you are running model trains in as near an authentic setting as possible, it is unfortunately not enough to have a beautiful off-the-shelf or scratch-built signalbox of the correct size and proportions for your track layout, apparently made of the appropriate materials and finished in the right colours, located in a spot where the signalman can access it, equipped with the appropriate mechanical and electrical equipment – a building from which your signalman can see how his signals have responded to the pulling and pushing of levers, and see the approaching and departing trains. In real life, signalboxes were always surrounded by certain indispensable ancillary features as important as the track was to locomotives and rolling stock. So, unless your model signalbox is in a display case, it will be necessary to include some of the following additional features.

One of the earliest pieces of regulation imposed by central government on railway companies was the fencing-off of all railway property, particularly track, to prevent the public from coming into contact with fast-moving and potentially deadly machines. In model form it is all too easy to forget about property boundaries, but if you want the setting of your signalbox to be right it will have to be fenced off from adjacent properties, public roads, etc [*see* **87**]. If you are modelling a traditional mechanical signalbox in a country setting, make sure it is within the boundary of railway-company property and does not share land with the neighbouring farmer; he would not be pleased [*see* **11**].

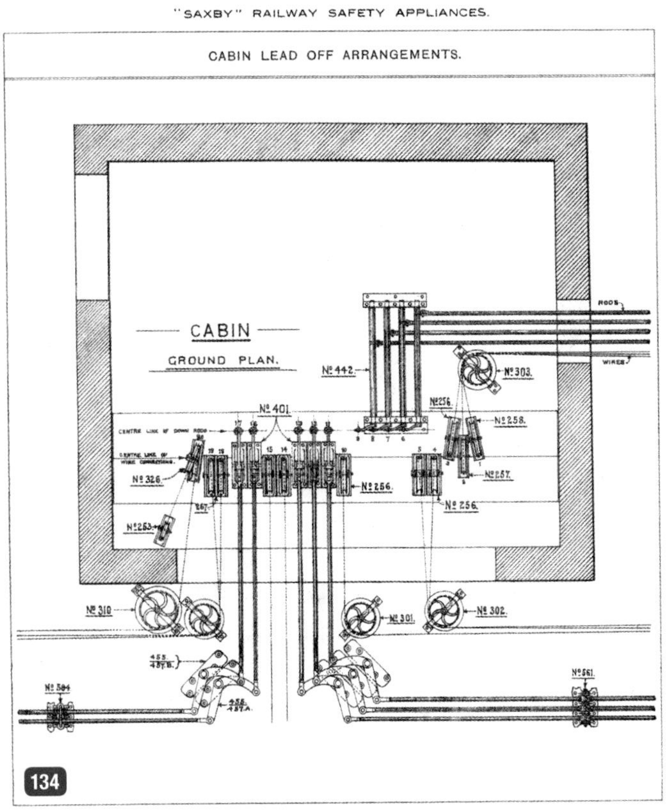

Until very recently signalboxes were not fenced off from the railway itself, so that signalmen always had direct access to the track. In the 19th and 20th centuries it was rare to find a gate separating a signalbox from a station platform. In the 21st century, however, with heightened concerns about security, it is now more common to find signalboxes in fenced enclosures, accessible only by padlocked or keypad-activated gates. Signalling centres (and now some traditional signalboxes in vulnerable locations) are also monitored by CCTV systems.

Until the 1960s it was not unusual to have a railway-owned cottage (or one in a terraced row) next to a signalbox, providing accommodation for the regular signalman. Remember that for most of the 19th century working men generally lived close to their place of work and that those who lived further away had either to walk or rely on public transport. Bicycles made a huge difference to the lives of ordinary working people when they appeared at the very end of the 19th century [*see* **38**]. After World War 2 motorised personal transport – first the moped or motor cycle, then the car – became more commonplace, and if you are setting your model in the early 21st century it will be appropriate to provide dedicated (and marked) parking spaces for your signalman and other Network Rail staff.

Long before widespread car ownership any special enclosure next to a signalbox would almost certainly have been used to store coal and dump waste ash from the fire. The walls of these bunkers would have been built of brick or formed of old sleepers, until prefabricated concrete became more usual just before and after World War 2. If you look carefully you will observe that many of the photographs in this book show various types of coal store.

Trimming and lighting signal lamps in the locking rooms of signalboxes was forbidden by most companies, and there are enough stories of signalboxes burning down when this rule was ignored to reveal how dangerous it could be. Until the introduction of long-burning lamps in the years immediately before World War 1 and their widespread adoption immediately afterwards (much later than most enthusiasts might presume) every signal lamp had to be taken down daily to be trimmed and filled. Consequently the separate lamp room was never far from every signalbox in the country, and many were used for their original purpose until well into the 1980s. They varied in form from substantial brick structures with pitched roofs [*see* **90**] to simple, prefabricated corrugated-iron sheds [*see* **22** and **43**].

Getting closer to the signalbox itself, if the style of structure you have chosen to model does not incorporate a toilet, modelling a small wooden or corrugated-tin shed near the coal store will give your model signalman some comfort during those long operating sessions. If your model is set in the post-Grouping or nationalised era you might provide a more substantial concrete hut, while if steam has vanished from the scene a Portaloo will be a necessity [*see* **84**].

LEFT A plan taken from a 1929 Westinghouse Brake & Saxby Signal Co catalogue. This 'typical' arrangement of wires and rods assumes a frame of 20 levers, Nos 1, 2, 3, 4, 5, 10, 14, 15, 18, 19 and 20 working signals, and Nos 6, 7, 8, 9, 11, 12, 13, 16 and 17 points/turnouts and/or facing-point locks. *Author's collection*

133

ABOVE The main distribution telegraph poles serving the ex-GNR signalbox on the East Coast main line at Abbotts Ripton remained in use until the 'box closed at the end of 1975. *Author*

At some locations on single lines, so that the signalman did not have either to lean out of a window or to walk down to the track to hand out or collect the token, signalboxes were provided with timber platforms which placed the locomotive crew and signalman on the same level [*see* **8**, **71**].

Another essential feature that really needs to be modelled is the main distribution telegraph pole – a continual presence from the 1860s to the 1960s. As the number of levers in a signalbox reflects the amount of lineside equipment to be worked, so the number of wires will indicate the complexity of the electrical equipment. One of Tyer & Co's major boasts in the 1870s was that its block instruments needed only a single wire to connect them between signalboxes, compared with the three wires required for those of other firms. Generally there were fewer wires between all signalboxes in the 19th century compared with the 20th century. The increasing use of signal and track-circuit repeaters, telephones and then, in BR days, the installation of block controls connected to lever functions (the electrical equivalent of Sykes 'lock and block') all added wires to the pole routes. Careful study of photographs will usually reveal whether you need to model single or double poles, the latter being preferred by the MR, for example.

Even when, from the 1970s, pole routes were replaced by heavily insulated cables running in concrete troughs, the main distribution pole often remained stubbornly in position [**133**], sometimes stripped of its arms, occasionally retaining them through lack of interest. A traditional mechanical signalbox without an adjacent telegraph pole is like a locomotive without its tender.

A common mid-20th-century intrusion near many signalboxes is the metal relay cabinet appearing in a number of sizes and either set on a concrete plinth [*see* **54**] or raised above the ground on concrete posts.

What always elevates the quality of any model signalbox is the representation of rods, wires, cranks and pulleys at the base of the structure. Rather as with block instruments, there can be confusion about exactly what is authentic in this area. Basically, wires connected signals to their operating levers, whilst rods operated the points/turnouts. Until well into the 1930s, the most common form of rods were wrought-iron and, later, steel tubes. By nationalisation these had been largely superseded by galvanised bars or channels, the shape of a lower-case 'n' in cross-section. The basic rule to remember is that there was usually one wire, rod or bar to work each piece of lineside equipment. If the locking mechanism of facing points was operated by a separate lever in the signalbox there would be two rods or bars going to that turnout. To change direction in a run of signal wire it was usual to insert a length of chain and run it around a cast-iron wheel, although cranks were

135

ABOVE One of the nicknames for the MSLR was 'money sunk and lost', but it is doubtful whether the company would have been so strapped for cash as to allow its buildings to end up looking like this. The metal sheeting affixed following an arson attack displayed this graffiti when the author photographed the signalbox in 1996; when he returned to photograph it again in the spring of 2010 the same graffiti was still there, any available money in the intervening 14 years having been spent on new security fencing and the inevitable CCTV cameras. *Author*

used in some locations. In a run of point rodding, cranks of various patterns were used to change direction [**134**]. Most of these items were bolted to balks of creosoted timber, although concrete supports became more common from the 1930s. Unfortunately the variety of mechanical equipment is too great to illustrate here, and modellers requiring more detailed information are advised to try to get hold of signalling contractors' catalogues.

Finally, the true finishing touches to any signalbox model, as with locomotives and rolling stock, will be the appropriate, weathered livery. It has proved impossible to assemble a complete list of all the colours signalboxes have been painted over the years, so the modeller is recommended to contact specialist historic railway societies for help in this area. As for weathering, unless the painters have only just left your signalbox and are walking down the lineside with ladder and buckets, then passing trains and the British weather will always leave their mark on the structure [*see* **61**]. The degree of weathering will depend largely on period and location. Generally speaking, the greatest care was lavished on all railway equipment, including signalboxes, during the Edwardian period. After that, standards gradually tailed off, only essential equipment maintenance being carried out during World War 2. Some pride did return in some places in the following years, but there were many signalboxes that met their ends in the 1960s and '70s still sporting traces of prewar paint [*see* **33**].

With regard to location, if your signalbox is set back from the running lines, and trains pass only slowly, there will be less 'track dirt' than if it is close to a section of fast main line. By contrast, a signalbox in a busy location could become very grimy indeed, especially if it was due to be replaced and as a consequence had received little or no attention [*see* **74**].

It was not always time or a lack of money that could leave its mark on signalboxes. Nesting birds and the habitual emptying of the teapot from one particular window by signalmen [*see* **17**] were other ways of staining the exterior, and from the 1960s there was always the risk of a graffiti attack [**135**]. But, so as not to end on a negative note, this does give the modeller an excuse to assemble a little troupe of men in either pre-1960s overalls or more modern high-visibility suits and hard-hats ready to give their signalbox a new coat of paint.